THE WORK CHALLENGE

THE WORK CHALLENGE

John Garnett

First published in April 1973 by
The Industrial Society
Peter Runge House
3 Carlton House Terrace
London SW1Y 5DG

Revised July 1974
Second Edition January 1978
Third Edition February 1981
Fourth Edition August 1985
Fifth Edition January 1988
Reprinted April 1988

ISBN 1 85091 570 9

© The Industrial Society

All rights reserved. No part of this publication may be reproduced, stored in a retrieval system or transmitted, in any form or by any means, electronic, mechanical, photocopying, recording, and/or otherwise without the prior written permission of the publisher. This book may not be lent, resold, hired out or otherwise disposed of by way of trade in any form, binding or cover other than that in which it is published, without prior consent of the publishers.

British Library Cataloguing in Publication Data

Garnett, John *1921*

The Work Challenge — 5th ed.
1. Job satisfaction
I. Title
658 3' 1422   HF5549 5 J63

Printed and bound in Great Britain by
Biddles Ltd, Guildford and King's Lynn

Contents

INTRODUCTION

CHAPTER	1	Why work matters	1
	2	Why is there a problem?	5
	3	The object and its achievement	13
	4	The work group leader	17
	5	Structure	21
	6	Leadership instruction, development and selection	29
	7	Targets and performance coaching	37
	8	Team Briefing	41
	9	Decision-taking	53
	10	Discipline	59
	11	Walking the job	65
	12	Job design	69
	13	Relevant conditions of employment	73
	14	Participative machinery	79
	15	Trade unions	87
	16	Young employees	93
	17	The common purpose	97
	18	Personal action	101
APPENDIX	1	Accountability chart – example	107
	2	Performance coaching – basic policy	109
	3	Performance coaching – simple form	110
	4	Understanding the economic facts – joint statement	111
	5	Management brief	116
	6	Decision taking	118
	7	Competitiveness with justice – joint statement	119
	8	Shop steward credentials	123
	9	Maximising human resources – checklist for organisations	124
	10	Practical participation	129
	11	The Industrial Society – objectives	132
	12	People who have influenced the author	136
INDEX			139

Introduction

Work has never been more important than it is today. Not only do we need the results of creative work so that we can pay for and develop our present society, but we shall only start to succeed in providing more jobs for people when we produce more effectively and profitably the goods and services people from across the world are prepared to buy.

There is a deep concern about unemployment and real fear of the results of technological change. Economic and social solutions of every kind are advocated, but success in practice will always depend on obtaining the involvement of all those who work in industry and commerce and their commitment to creating the goods and services. Those who work in the public service also have a vital part to play by achieving more with less through using their resources more sparingly and with greater efficiency.

This book outlines the problems of obtaining the fullest commitment of people to their work; it details the known answers. Most important of all it is concerned with what each one of us must do to make it happen in practice. The book is short to save the time of those who manage and of trade unionists who represent. The practical examples should illustrate the points better than pages of theory. Every effort has been made to find the simplest answers in the belief that the ultimate truths are simple, and in the knowledge that only relatively simple procedures have any hope of being made to work.

The recommended actions are firstly from personal experience of working at every level, from clerk to more senior management in a large company, and observing the actions of the most effective managers and supervisors. Then from being appointed the Director of The Industrial Society, which now employs 260 people, and helping to increase its earnings 40-fold to £6½ million in 23 years. And finally from working with many of the 16,000 member organisations of The Industrial Society during these happy years.

The book is dedicated to all my dear colleagues and to those who have inspired me during that time.

JOHN GARNETT
April 1985

1 Why work matters

Making work more worthwhile is the challenge of our age. The need to work in industry and commerce is questioned and yet people's commitment to work is vital to the future of the community. Everything we have – whether it be hospitals, food, schools or housing, and all that we wish to achieve in improving the living standards of older people, housing the homeless or helping feed much of the world – depends on the effective creation of goods and services.

We in Britain are compassionate. Whatever people's political persuasion they mostly want to do good whether it is keeping open some local hospital, reducing the size of classes, improving the environment or helping the disabled. However, the achievement of these good things depends on the ability to create the wherewithal to pay for them. There are those who believe we should borrow forward; in other words we should consume goods and services which have to be paid for by our children and our grandchildren. We maintain our standard of living at the expense of work to be done by future generations. All of us know at heart that we do not have the right to do this and must pay our own way. It is the same with creating jobs. Government job creation programmes can help by lessening the evils of unemployment. But unemployment will only be significantly reduced when our goods and services are in such demand across the world because of their quality, record of prompt delivery and effectiveness.

Example

A company in the Oxford area which started with one person now employs more than 500 because the ingenuity and quality of its product have resulted in worldwide sales. They are even able to compete successfully in Japan because their after sale service is better than that of another organisation creating a similar product in Japan.

The need to create work through successful enterprise is of paramount importance. Neville Shute, writing about the 1930s, summed it up so well:

> 'The cure is for somebody to buckle to and make a job for three people. I believe that is the thing most worth doing in this modern world. To create a job that people can work at and be proud of and make money by doing their work.'

It is primarily a matter of harnessing the ingenuity, enthusiasm and gifts that are present in all of us to create the things people need. The opportunity lies with all of us whose job it is to obtain the co-operation of others at work.

For the individual, lack of commitment and involvement in work is a great loss. Work is a necessary part of human life and it is tragic that so many people get so little satisfaction from it. Hospitals and mental homes have more people in them who are utterly frustrated with their work than those who are overburdened with it.

A measure of the challenge is to be seen in the vastly greater number of days we lose each year in sickness absence than in industrial disputes. This sickness absence is largely a measure of our failure to get people to realise that they and their work matter.

It is illustrated by remarks made in local authorities and government agencies:

> 'I'm taking off three days before Christmas because I haven't used up my sickness entitlement.'

And in a commercial office by a woman still at lunch half an hour after the lunch hour ended:

> 'And when I go back late I only wish that someone would care.'

It is evident in the secretaries who leave because they do not have enough to do, and in the factory workers whose abilities are not used, in the graduate trainees in banks and engineering companies who look to other jobs because they are underused.

It is not a question of people not wanting to work. The general complaint of all who have been employed up to middle management level in large organisations is of being underused, underemployed, frustrated and unable to bring their gifts to bear.

Example

When asking fitters in a machine shop what I should say to the board and senior management, whom I was to address 20 minutes later, they said: 'Tell them that we really do know a bit about engineering and fitting and would so like to contribute our ideas and skills more usefully.'

This is not a problem which is affected by the ownership of the organisation. It is as great in government, nationalised industries and hospitals, as it is in independent enterprise.

The provision of satisfying leisure is no alternative to worthwhile work. People argue about the difference between work and leisure. Perhaps the most helpful definition is that leisure is for oneself; work is service to others.

The gifts of ingenuity, energy, enthusiasm and technical ability are there in all of us. The problem is to get these abilities committed to the task.

Are we in Britain behind the rest of the world in solving the problem of commitment to work? No, we are probably ahead of many other countries in the problems we are tackling. As other countries increasingly give people the kind of security, expectation, freedom and rights which we have achieved in Britain, they will also experience the difficulties of getting people to pay as much attention to duties as to rights.

So many of the solutions of other countries are the ones we applied years ago. Many of Japan's methods of motivation are those used in this country 70 and 80 years ago. When one observes attitudes to work in the USA or Germany, it is interesting to note how much they have in common with past decades in Britain.

The clock cannot be put back. We can, however, restrain ourselves from demanding more rights until we have learned to pay for the ones we already have. And we can strive during these last 20 years of the twentieth century to pioneer ways of getting free men and women to co-operate to produce the goods and services on which the community's future depends. This is the challenge.

2 Why is there a problem?

There are many reasons why the problem of getting people's commitment to work has become widespread in recent years. The main ones are:

Size

There is really no difficulty for an employer, with a bit of enthusiasm and by setting a good example, to get a small group – say less than 20 – working to its highest potential. It is quite different in organisations with between 100 and 100,000 employees, where there may be up to twelve levels of management between where a decision is taken and where it is carried out. In large organisations it is too easy to feel like a cog in a wheel.

Example

In one large company there were 87 people sitting in the distribution department in an open office. The company did what it could, by spending large sums on a magazine telling people they were not cogs in a wheel. But each individual could see the other 86 cogs sitting round the department.

Of course, small is beautiful, but it is no good arguing that people should only work in small organisations. If the community is to benefit from the savings of size in technology, integration of effort and financial strength, it is necessary to have a large number of people together in one organisation. The computer industry, for instance, requires a large number of people to work together; but size makes it difficult for individuals to feel that they matter.

High technology and investment in machines mean people must work around the clock. It is all too easy to forget the night shift. A minister, preaching on Christmas day, made the point: 'In telling the shepherds first it was so typical of the Almighty to tell the night shift first.'

Much work is not self-motivating

If the community is to benefit from specialisation many jobs will be dull and repetitive. Some of the new jobs can be worse than the ones they replace. It was always difficult to motivate a clerk to take information off invoices accurately and post it in ledgers. To motivate someone to punch information on to data processing cards at 22,000 depressions an hour is more difficult. Keeping on your toes when watching numerically controlled machines may be more difficult than directly operating those machines, which at least keeps you physically involved.

People's expectations from work

People's expectations from work are much higher than in the past. It is not just a question of earning money: they want to be involved and to participate. They have grown up in schools where they can affect decisions and where authority is questioned and explanations are expected.

Example

Talking to a seven-year-old, he told me he had written a five-sided letter to the teacher of his five-year-old sister, explaining that the teacher was not teaching his sister to read adequately. His sister was not on advanced enough books and didn't have enough homework.

It never apparently occurred to him that the teacher might tell him to mind his own business, or not to be cheeky. And he was not in the least surprised to receive one and a half pages, in type, answering the points he had made.

Despite unemployment many young people are not prepared to do some of the jobs available. Either they are too badly paid or they believe the jobs are beneath their abilities. They are not so prepared as their parents and grandparents were to move to the South East where jobs are available.

In the commercial and computer world people are inclined to change jobs. It is argued by some that the new generation does not have the loyalty of past generations. The fact is, the situation has changed. The opportunity for movement to other comparable jobs is greater. If men and women read the advertisements in the Sunday papers and see how much greener the grass is in every other job their loyalty will be under strain on Monday morning.

The Welfare State

Since 1945 real efforts have been made by successive British governments to provide state benefits to remove the worst aspects of insecurity and need. This in turn has reduced some of the older incentives to work. Most people agree that, although it can produce problems, removing extreme forms of need is socially desirable. Whichever party is in power this attitude is likely to continue in Britain for some time. It is also something other countries aim for increasingly.

In recent years we have had eleven Acts of Parliament giving people more working rights, security, equal pay, equal opportunity, trade union protection, provision of information and much else.

Management can no longer rely on people's fear of being out of a job as the final deterrent. As a chairman of a major company said: 'It really is quite a challenge to manage in a country where they have abolished the stick and the carrot by legislation'. For the majority of people we have achieved the Christian (and Marxist) aim of 'unto each according to his need'. It is, however, much more difficult to achieve the other half of the philosophy 'from each according to his ability'.

Example

It was fascinating to hear an American personnel director of a subsidiary company in this country say that as his parent company in the States knew all about management, they didn't need any help in the UK. But he did think it a bit odd that the community should 'subsidise' strikes through state aid! It is, of course, just because such things can happen in a socially advanced country that there is a problem of getting people to recognise the importance of work.

The miners' strike of 1984 has shown how people can survive without earnings from work and without strike pay from the union for a very long time. The sanctions of starvation are no longer available, thank goodness, but it does mean there is a real challenge in getting people to act responsibly and to recognise their duties as well as their rights.

Shortage of 'ready-made' recruits

In days past there seemed to be plenty of able people to fill the necessary jobs. We hear now, even in times of unemployment, that organisations are finding it difficult to recruit the kind of self-motivated people they need.

Example

A brewery in Wiltshire reported that the calibre of people applying for jobs wasn't what it used to be. Things have changed from the days when country people would queue up to work in the brewery. There is no doubt that with better education the ability is there, but it needs bringing out; it no longer happens of its own accord.

There are those who believed the fear of unemployment would be a great motivator to high performance. However, the last few years have proved the exact opposite to be true. Unemployment tends to discourage people from co-operating with change or working any harder in case they work themselves or their colleagues out of a job.

Money alone will not buy high performance

People work for money and most people, however much they have, want more of it. But money alone will not buy high performance in terms of quality, customer service, flexibility and restraint in demands. Employers who by piecework, bonuses and commission have tried to buy high performance have failed in the long run. Such cash incentives can produce short-term results, but a bonus scheme, once installed, becomes a fining scheme – people have their money docked for failure to achieve. This results in defensive attitudes, increased resistance to change and a disinclination to work to capacity in order to leave something in hand.

An increasing number of companies have moved away from piecework to measured day-work, stepped incentives or salary-type payments. Where fluctuating bonus schemes have been clung to, they have led to unending disputes about money, rather than discussions about how to do the job better. Bonus schemes have also become increasingly irrelevant and impractical when applied to new types of jobs. Even the most sophisticated schemes have been sidestepped by employees who have a great deal more time to think about getting round the scheme than management has to think about filling the loopholes.

In a country such as Britain where there is a high commitment to compassion, tax levels will remain high and any financial rewards will thereby be eroded. For all these reasons money alone is not as effective as it used to be in obtaining high commitment to work.

The changing role of the unions

Unions are concerned with the success of the enterprise in the interest of their members, but they cannot be held responsible for getting the necessary high performance from employees.

In years gone by many managements were able to get the central union officials to play a major part in getting work from their members. If an agreement had been signed giving the company the right to expect a particular level of performance, full-time union officials would have a go at their members. This concept of the union managing its members is becoming increasingly unrealistic. The power no longer lies with union officials. The union is not a management body or a subcontractor of labour. It is a representative body where, in the last resort, the members own the union, not vice versa.

This fact of life is crucial when considering ideas about participation. It is quite unrealistic to believe that, because union representatives participate in policy decisions, they can be held accountable for executing those decisions – or even, single-handed, communicating them. It is not their job to 'get it out the door'.

The power structure in unions is moving all the time towards an inverted pyramid shape as shown in diagram 1:

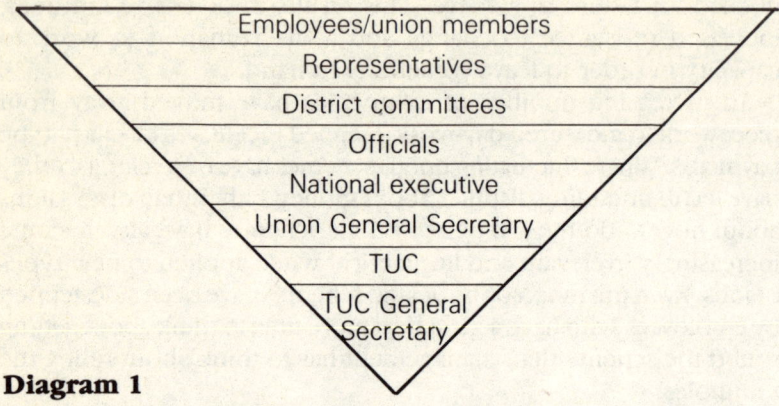

```
Employees/union members
    Representatives
    District committees
        Officials
    National executive
  Union General Secretary
         TUC
      TUC General
        Secretary
```

Diagram 1

In the final analysis the union must respect the views of the active members. It is, however, worth noting that all the trade union members who ultimately own the unions (not vice versa) are employed many hours a week by employers. We too frequently blame the unions for the lack of co-operation of employees. We are inclined to talk about the 'union members' when people do not co-operate and about the 'employees' when they do. They are one and the same people.

Increasingly, success depends upon persuading people to co-operate. This is an operation for winning the minds and hearts of people, and so the earlier diagram can be complemented with a second pyramid, as in diagram 2.

```
       Management
        influence
           ▼
   Employees/union members
           ▼
      Representatives
      Union officials
           TUC
```

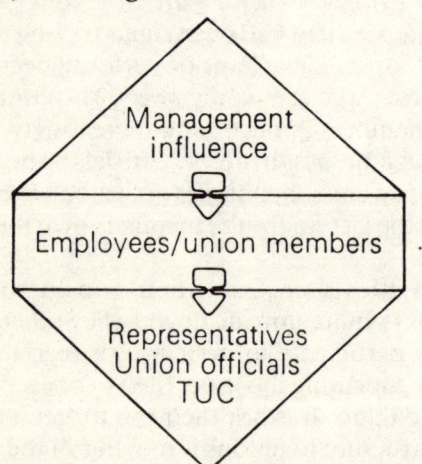

Diagram 2

Company welfare

Company welfare schemes are not as effective as they once were in encouraging work and commitment. Forty years ago many people worked hard for the more enlightened companies because they appreciated the basic welfare that their company was providing at a time when it was not available from the state. Nowadays, raising welfare above an adequate level is likely to be counter-productive.

Example
A company which fitted plush carpets into their already adequate offices in an effort to improve co-operation, found their staff did not see the need to work particularly hard if the company could afford this kind of luxury.

Denigration of leadership

Another major problem is that not enough attention has been paid to the vital role of the leader at every level. Everyone with working experience knows the importance of the immediate boss, whether that person is a supervisor, the manager, the headmistress, the under secretary or the managing director. Yet, in spite of the importance of leaders, their activities have been much denigrated.

For many, leadership seems to be synonymous with authoritarianism, close supervision, the squirarchy, paternalism, 'officer-like qualities', class privilege, and for some even totalitarianism. In rejecting these concepts of leadership we seem to have thrown away the baby with the bathwater and failed to recognise the vital role of relevant leadership.

The leader's job is to call forth the gifts of people and help them to work for a common task. It is a job of getting the team to work together rather than damage itself by internal conflict. It is helping people to rise to their highest potential and freeing them from restrictions. If we look at sport, who would even attempt to win a team game without a playing captain? The working leader is vital.

In recent years a generation of young people have grown up who, through no fault of their own, seem to have been taught to challenge every aspect of the system that has been built up, and the very existence of a socially desirable role for leaders. At times it looks as though their teachers had muddled anarchy with freedom and taught them to believe that society can be helped by people contracting-out and not becoming involved.

Whereas, of course, the truth does not lie here at all. The role for the idealist or caring men and women is to get involved and make industry and commerce and all society a better place in the interests of all.

3 THE OBJECT AND ITS ACHIEVEMENT

Having looked at the main difficulties in getting people involved in their work we now turn to what needs to be done to overcome these difficulties in practice.

The common purpose of industry and commerce must be the creation of the goods and services that the community needs, and to do this with a profit or a surplus. More is said about this common purpose in Chapter 17. In the case of the public service it must be to meet the needs of the people they serve with the minimum use of resources.

A major part of achieving this purpose depends on the people in the organisation. The objective can be expressed in a number of ways. Perhaps the simplest is: that each of us should give of our best to our work. The advantage of this definition is that nobody can be complacent because it is almost unachievable. Another definition is: the fullest involvement of people so that they may put more into and get more out of their work. Yet another is: the best use of the gifts in people.

Before dealing with the most effective methods of achieving these objectives we ought first to consider the morality behind them. How do we answer accusations that we are simply using people as 'profit fodder', exploiting and manipulating them, involving them to the extent that they are wrecked by the rat race of material life, or sacrificing personality to the organisation?

Leadership differs from manipulation in that leaders will be totally open in their endeavours to persuade people to co-operate for given objectives. Manipulators will pull their strings and usually deny they are doing so. The main case for leadership, however, must be concerned with ends as well as means. What is the moral right of using the gifts of people and involving people in creative endeavours?

At the most senior level, men and women may become too involved with their work at the expense of other responsibilities, including family life. However, the dangers of allowing oneself to be an 'organisation man' and of being caught up in a rat race are not restricted to industry and commerce. Wherever there are large organisations, be they in government, teaching or hospitals, there can be such problems.

Many of us form early the belief that there is a major conflict between efficiency and the interests of people. However, those of us who have worked in large organisations are forced to recognise that people prefer to work for leaders who get the most from them rather than for those who, by striving after happiness, end up protecting people and frustrating them.

Personnel managers who see their jobs in terms of protecting staff are often amazed to note how people ask to transfer to departments where the boss works the staff hard. The human problem at work for most people is being under-involved and feeling that their gifts of intelligence, ingenuity and energy are not required.

Example

A technical manager repeatedly had success with people wherever he was managing whether in research, technical service, production or sales. His section, a major department, achieved results, they succeeded where others failed, people worked late and at weekends when the task demanded it. As the personnel manager of the organisation, I expected to receive requests from people to move out of the department because they were being exploited. In practice I only received requests from people asking to move into the department because working for this particular boss was fun. He delegated to you, he trusted you, he got you to achieve things you did not think you were capable of doing.

Perhaps St Thomas Aquinas understood the frustration of most people at work when he pointed out 700 years ago that it was immoral to misuse people, underuse them and abuse them, but that it was highly moral to call forth and make use of the gifts that were in people. It is also certain that people will not use their gifts to the benefit of the organisation unless they are treated as people with all the needs that people have.

The objective of involving people in work is both morally and socially desirable. But how is it to be achieved? Not, to be sure, through any one answer – be it called participation, management by objectives, team briefing or organisation development.

It is equally unrealistic to hold that if a particular set of management actions are carried out there will be no need to do anything about management-union relations: that 'if you manage well unions will go away'. Any effective answers must cover the role of managers *and* unions.

A number of actions are needed if people are to get going. All these different actions must, however, integrate into a whole, otherwise the policies will be self-contradictory. If the importance of the supervisor is stressed under the heading of structure then it will not do to set up a system of communication that ignores that person's presence.

The actions that need to be taken will have the following features:

1 They will integrate into one whole designed to achieve the best ('the 100') from people. For an illustration of this see diagram 3.

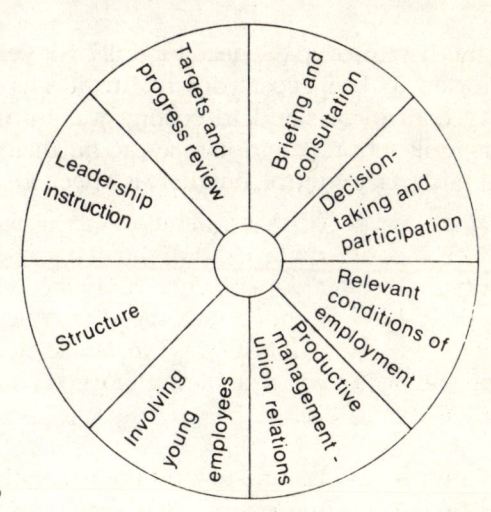

Diagram 3

2 The answers must be practical and simple. Time is at a premium and there is much to do besides involving people. Simple answers are necessary to make things happen in practice.

3 The aim is for the 'least worst' way of doing things. Nothing will work perfectly, but some things will work a great deal better than others. Under the law of diminishing returns 20 per cent of the effort usually produced 80 per cent of the results. Organisations need to set minimum requirements in each of these areas which their subsidiary units or departments must meet. However, they should allow flexibility on how these requirements are met.
4 All solutions involve the word 'normally'. There will always be exceptions, but these should not amount to more than 15 per cent of the rule.
5 The actions should be designed on the expectation that they will be successful for 85 per cent of people. People cannot be divided between co-operative and unco-operative, effective or ineffective. Any group of people are spread on a Gaussian distribution, 15 per cent are co-operative, 15 per cent are not, but 70 per cent can be influenced one way or the other.
6 The right attitude without a simple monitorable drill will not be effective, nor vice versa.

Example

Accountants have proved the need for drills. For years everyone was exhorted to keep costs down. But it was only when budgetary control or standard costing was introduced that managers took action. You don't have to be an accountant to carry out budgetary control, but there is a need for the routine.

4 The work group leader

As other motivators become less effective, the role of the work group leader becomes increasingly important. Whether these people are called chargehands in a factory, section leaders in an office, or tutors in a college, it is their ability to get people to co-operate or give more of themselves to their work which becomes the crucial factor. Most of us know this from our own experience. When we look back over the years and consider the key factor in whether we moved nearer or further away from the ideal of giving our best, we realise this depended primarily on who at any given time was our boss. One boss would delegate to us, let us get on with the job, allow us to have a sense of achievement, give us credit for what we had done and remind us of the importance of what we were doing. Another boss failed to do these things.

The importance of the immediate leader is confirmed when you look at an organisation from a senior manager's point of view. You notice that in a particular person's group there are few problems: that person gets results; there are no problems with the union; the leader holds the staff. By contrast in other groups under different leaders there are continual difficulties, even though the overall situation is identical.

Example

A company with high absence and lateness rates, after trying all other methods, made it clear that absence was regarded as the responsibility of the immediate leader of the work group, and the absence and lateness figures were published against the name of the leader of each group. Within weeks the figures improved as never before.

One of the great retail stores knows the importance of this

same point. They publish to all employees each week the sales results against the name of the store manager and, within the store, against the name of each departmental head.

The introduction of procedures for participation does not in any way lessen the importance of the role of the work group leader. The participation of representatives in contributing to decisions does not ensure that these decisions will be carried out. It is the job of the executive, the manager and the immediate leader to make it happen and to persuade all concerned to co-operate to their best ability.

There are those who would argue theoretically that there is no need for a team leader or, alternatively, that the leader could be the same as the shop steward.

I remember a debate between the chairman of a great company and an outstanding trade union leader. The former argued that with a good foreman, or section leader, you did not need a shop steward. Foremen or supervisors should never be representatives of the people for whom they are accountable.

The immediate leaders must be the foreman, chargehand or section leader. The importance of the foreman has been stressed frequently in the past. Nothing like the same attention has been paid to the section leader in offices. And recently even the foreman has been neglected as functional departments, such as work study and quality control, have become more important. All the talk of participation is concerned with even more involvement of shop stewards or elected representatives but little is said about the systematic involvement of supervisors. Unceasing attention has been given by consultants and others to organisation and structure at the top. But the main people management problem lies at the bottom and no such attention has been given at this level. At the lowest level people frequently do not know who is their boss.

Example

In a highly sophisticated company practising an advanced form of behavioural science at the top, there were grave doubts as to who was responsible for whom at the work-group level. Three operators were asked who was their boss. One said it was the foreman, another said it was the quality control supervisor and the third said it was the shop steward. The management said it was the section leader who was in charge of them.

Example

In a great engineering company a design engineer with 22 years' service was asked who was his boss. He replied: 'That is a fascinating question; they call it matrices management but we call it chaos.' Of course in large complicated organisations there has to be an inter-relationship between functional departments, line departments and projects. But at any given moment it needs to be crystal clear who is responsible for whom. We talk of accountability for expenditure and finance but who is accountable for the individual people, the most valuable asset of all?

Example

In a famous company on the Clyde, since bankrupt, I recall asking a number of workers who was their boss. They asked what I meant. I said who was the person whose job it was to achieve their co-operation, set them targets, consult and communicate with them. 'Ah,' they replied, 'we don't have any of those.'

It has often been said that people are as good as their boss makes them. There is a great deal of truth in that and it is therefore necessary to decide who is the boss of whom.

The supervisory structure at the lowest levels has normally been decided by the technical content of the job. If a fitter was lining up a turbine then there was a supervisor because it was a technically difficult job; the same principle applied in offices. If the job was simple and repetitive a supervisor might be responsible for 40 or more people. These arrangements may have been adequate when other factors motivated people. Now, when the co-operation and involvement of people is so crucial to profitability and efficiency, we need to pay attention to the numbers of people responsible to every leader at every level of the organisation, and to check the structure *from the bottom up* as well as from the top down.

5 Structure

The structure must clarify who is each person's immediate leader. It must show who is accountable for involving people at each and every level. In the case of a changing or evolving structure it is even more important that at any given time people are clear about who is their boss. In deciding on the structure there are some general rules that are worth applying.

The pyramid

The most effective form of structure for any organisation that must achieve results is the pyramid. In this a leader is responsible for a team and each of those people is responsible for a team and so on through the organisation. Highly successful chairmen of great organisations have said that the sweep of history has shown this is the way to achieve results. There are many forms of structure to achieve the consensus of policy but when it comes to getting things done there must be a leader and a team at each level throughout the organisation. Pyramidal structures are frequently described as authoritarian or hierarchical by those who oppose them. Such structures can, however, be operated in a supportive, participative and enabling manner. Some would suggest that people are freer without structure; the opposite is the case. Where each of us has a clear area to work in with a designated team leader we have more freedom.

Technical leadership and the leadership of people should not be divided

It is no good having a section leader who hands out the work and a departmental head who sees people about their salaries or whenever there is trouble.

After the First World War there was a theory that this divided responsibility could work – you could have an ex-rugby international as personnel manager who would be 'good with the lads', thus allowing the engineer or chemist to get on with the technical job. It was soon discovered that you couldn't run a job effectively when it was divided like this. The quality of engineering was a factor in getting the team to contribute to the job. The person in charge of the job was in charge of the people on the job.

Yet at the lowest levels of management we still find this split of function. Too frequently foremen or departmental heads consider themselves responsible for discipline while the chargehand or section leader hands out the work.

A simple test to see if leaders are in charge of their people is to ask them if they consider themselves responsible when members of their team are absent and whether the team considers it part of their job to do something about it. If the answer to this is no, and the leader is inclined to lay the responsibility on others, it is clear that person does not realise they are in charge of the group.

The size of the work group

The person who is the leader must have no more than 15 people reporting to them, however simple the task. This is the maximum number of individuals that a team leader can expect to involve and, furthermore, if working groups are allowed to become larger it is impossible for people to participate. Those who have run meetings will know the difference between the success of a meeting with 14 round the table rather than 24. The figure of 14/15 people is not an average and therefore any calculation which results from dividing the number of supervisors into the total number of employees is irrelevant.

The point is, no team should have more than 15 people responsible to one person. It may be that if the task is complicated the numbers will need to be fewer. (We talk a lot about 'team spirit' but the largest team is in rugby union. Even in that game it is difficult to keep the forwards and backs together particularly after losing a match.) Much that goes wrong at work is due to the large number of people responsible to an immediate leader. When asked to investigate an industrial relations problem the first question I ask is about the size of the work group and the numbers responsible to the immediate boss. When asking such a question in a large engineering company the dialogue went as follows:

Questioner: *How many people are you responsible for?*

Foreman: *Seventy-two with two progress-chasers to help me, but they are not in charge of people.*

Questioner: *In that case how do you treat people as individuals, consult them, communicate with them, set them targets?*

Foreman: *How would you?*

Questioner: *I wouldn't.*

Foreman: *I don't.*

Example

In a hospital where healing and the number of available beds was lessened by the loss of cleaning staff, the size of work groups was reduced to teams of fourteen people, each with a working leader. Within two months the hospital was able to retain its full complement of cleaners for the first time in six years.

A major part of a company manufacturing wires and cables reduced their production costs by cutting the size of the work group to no more than thirteen women to what they called a 'mother hen'.

If groups are kept sufficiently small, the leader will have time to do other things. In a transport department if there is to be one supervisor for fifteen to eighteen drivers, what will the supervisor do when the drivers are out? The best answer seems to be to consider using a senior driver, who will work as a driver for some of the time and also carry out the leadership function for the team of drivers. Another method is to use functional bosses, such as inspectors on bus routes, and to give them the additional job of being responsible for the leadership of fifteen to eighteen drivers.

Example

French Railways have developed a new person called the *chef de traction*. This person is the working leader of a small team of designated drivers. Besides driving, the *chef de traction* also spends time with the drivers in the team.

In the past, we have been inclined to get rid of working bosses – the chargehands – particularly on the factory floor, because they spent too much time working and not enough managing. However, in offices it has always been normal for the manager to work and manage and lead a team. The problem of not paying enough attention to the leadership part of the job can be overcome by setting targets of the leadership actions required.

Increasingly, organisations are recognising the vital role of working leaders, whether they are inspectors on the railways, the chargeman in a coal mine, a supervisor in the civil service or the section leader in commerce.

Example

Baggage handling has improved markedly since the baggage handling manager was replaced with a number of working team leaders. Instead of the manager saying: 'Go and unload that aircraft', the working team leader says: 'Come and unload that aircraft'.

People in work pools

The nature of some work makes it necessary for people to work under different bosses. Examples are audit clerks who will work in different groups, research officers joining project teams, craftsmen out on different jobs. In these cases there are great advantages in allocating individuals to one of the team leaders so that, although they may be working at any particular moment with one of the other team leaders, they know who is their regular boss.

In the same way, in a machine shop with a foreman and chargehand it is far more effective for some of the group to be allocated to the foreman and some to the chargehand, even though people may work at any given moment for either. In the case of shift working, shifts must stick with a regular shift leader.

Another complication arises where a pool of people is needed to increase the staffing of various jobs depending on day-to-day needs.

Example

One food company has found that rather than start people in the 'pool' at the beginning of their employment, it works better to put new people under a regular supervisor and only promote them to the pool if they are seen to be particularly self-reliant. The pool in this company is looked on as a high-calibre commando where its members can work anywhere, and pool members receive a premium rate of pay because of their flexibility.

Not too small

There is a tendency higher up in organisations to have too few people reporting to the level above. People who have worked in the middle grades well know that one of the reasons they could not give of their best was that the person above them was always doing their job for them. Part of the reason for this is because each of these senior levels did not have enough people reporting to them.

If you have only a deputy and two assistants reporting to you, it is perfectly possible, with a little energy, to do all their jobs as well as your own. If, however, you have seven people reporting to you the structure encourages you to delegate or collapse.

Working groups will therefore be most effective at every level when they consist of between four and fifteen people.

Deputies are best avoided

Deputies muddle the accountability and people are not clear who is their leader. Those who have worked under deputies will know the problem of writing a paper which has the support of the deputy, but is turned down by the boss, or vice versa. This bolstering of a person's failings by a deputy to try to make two half-people into one whole person blocks up the mechanism. Dual accountability creates more levels, more delays and less delegation.

It is important, however, that at each level one of the team is labelled as 'acting in the absence of' the person above when that person is away. No delays need then occur and the necessary decisions are made.

The fewer levels the better

Although organisations can never be tidy it is worth noting that if the head of the unit has seven people reporting, and each of those people has seven, and at the lowest level there are twelve people to each leader, this makes an organisation of 588 people with only three levels of leadership.

Go for operational management

Though it must be absolutely clear who is accountable for the performance of each person, there may well be a balance of arguments between whether the people concerned should be accountable to their functional boss, or to their operational boss. For example, should the local accountant be responsible to the manager of that location or to the chief accountant of the organisation at head office? Should sales executives be accountable to the chief sales director or to the general manager of the unit for which they are selling? How do we get the best of both worlds? While the arguments are balanced, the guiding factor should be: what is the objective of the particular operation and where does the profit or cost centre lie?

Example

When deciding whether to keep shift fitters reporting to the maintenance day engineer or to put them under the shift process foreman, the key point should be: are we in the business of maintaining plants or are we producing and selling a product? If this argument is followed, shift fitters should be responsible to the process shift foreman but they will have a dotted line relationship to the maintenance engineer and chief engineer.

This argument causes alarm in the professional engineering world, and among some unions, where the idea of a skilled person reporting to a process supervisor seems sacrilege. But it is only common sense and works best that way.

Where teams or departments are growing there is a temptation to bolster heads of department by giving them perhaps a training supervisor and a work study person. It is more effective to use such people as subsidiary team leaders although one of them could still have the responsibility for quality across the department.

Example

The sewing department in a luggage manufacturers had grown in 20 years from ten to 60 people, and the job of managing the unit had become impossible. The company gave the leader a quality control assistant and two training assistants. It would have been more effective if they had split the team among these three people each being totally responsible for fifteen.

The ship system

So far, the examples of operational management have applied to the shop floor or office floor level. When this principle is applied at organisational levels, it is often called the ship system. Is it better to put all marketing and sales people of an organisation together under one section, with production under another and accountancy under a third or is it better to make the local accountant report to the manager of that location with a dotted line relationship to the group chief accountant? When some consultants are asked advice on this subject they tend to suggest to organisations which are organised functionally to organise themselves operationally and vice versa. The rule of thumb is to follow the profit centre. The key to effective organisation is to arrange things so the person whose job it is to take a decision can embrace all the necessary functions and be at the lowest level. This avoids having to refer every little thing to the highest level before a decision can be taken. It is the concept of it being easier in a small ship to gain the commitment of every individual to the task than in a large ship. Working on the ship concept, the number of people under any general manager should be kept to less than 500. There is much evidence that this is the effective size of unit, whether in industry, commerce, or the public service. It used to be thought that this was because the boss of the unit could know 500 people by name. I think the reason for this figure is that a unit of 500 allows every team leader (say 40) to know and be known intimately by the overall boss.

The concept of matrices management whereby a person is equally accountable to a function and to the operation has been much advocated by theorists. It is, of course, a marvellous way of getting out of deciding who is accountable to whom. It may be attractive in concept when looking down from above, but at the point of work it causes unending argument, manoeuvring, manipulation and politicking. I note that the great chairmen who have thought it through and have survived will have none of it. There is, of course, a dotted line and a thick line in organisations of any size. There is function and operation, staff and line but the key to success is to decide where the thick line lies – who is accountable for the motivation and involvement of each individual?

Accountability charts

To force senior managers to clarify who is accountable for whom and to make them ensure that each person knows who is their immediate leader, there is real value in producing accountability charts. These are far more effective for this purpose than the normal organisational charts. Organisational charts, with their use of colours, dotted lines, boxes, and even three dimensions, may show some complex inter-relationships but they fail to bring out the key accountability for individuals at each level.

The advantage of an accountability chart is that it crystallises who is accountable for getting the best co-operation from each individual. (See Appendix 1.) The other advantage of an accountability chart is that it is in alphabetical order and does not show status. Reference to status often leads to unending trouble. Everybody in the organisation should be given the page or pages of the accountability chart that show where they fit in who is their boss and who is their boss's boss. In organisations which are changing to meet new needs it is more, not less, important to have a clear accountability chart even if it has to be changed frequently.

6 Leadership instruction, development and selection

Has every person in a leadership job, at every level in the organisation, had some practical instruction in what they must do to involve their people and get them to participate so they can give their best to their work?

Instruction

Experience has repeatedly shown that people's leadership abilities can be improved by practical training. For the last 50 years, industry and commerce have had the advantage of employing large numbers of people who had leadership experience and training in the armed forces. Those who were involved in either of the two world wars received their experience in the services, while those who remained behind assumed responsibilities at an earlier age than they would have in peace time. Now this ready trained pool of leaders is no longer available. The need for industry and commerce to do their own instruction in leadership is therefore more important than ever before.

The instruction must concentrate on what effective leaders *do*, not on what they need to be. The object is not to change an introvert into an extrovert. The leader can be just as effective as one or the other. Nor are we concerned with making all people the same. What we need to ensure is that, in their own way, they carry out certain leadership activities.

There is no evidence that lectures on leadership qualities or styles will, in themselves, encourage those qualities in people. Lectures on integrity don't give people more integrity by the end of the session. It is possible, however, to train people to do what a person with integrity would do, and as a result of doing these things the qualities are developed.

Example

If young managers say they cannot go out and talk to people about their problems because they would not be sincere, the answer is:

'Don't worry about feeling sincere, just go and talk to people about their problems because that is part of your job as a manager; you will become sincere soon enough when you learn what their problems are.'

Leadership instruction must also be reproducible and suitable for ordinary managers to teach – there are a vast number of people in leadership positions who need to be trained and too few so-called experts to cover them.

When deciding on the form of training beware of anything which concentrates on analysing people's problems ('paralysis by analysis'). People need help to find and apply answers. They will be helped by instruction.

Example

It does not improve a supervisor to be told the psychological problems of giving someone an instruction. It may in fact only make the supervisor more self-conscious. What leaders need to know is how, in difficult circumstances and with a shortage of time, they can get people to carry out a decision with enthusiasm.

Leadership instruction is more effective when it is post-experience, ie after people have been in a leadership job for six months, so that they know something of the problems and pressures.

One form of training which can be reproduced and is based on the action a leader needs to take is called Action-Centred Leadership training. It has evolved from some original work by John Adair. More details are given in Appendix 2, but the key is to build the instruction round the three overlapping actions of the leader: achieve the task, build the team, develop individuals. (See diagram 4).

The training can be given by anyone who has had some leadership experience. It is better if the leader has attended a brief course, but the concept is simple and straightforward.

A small team of five is formed from those being trained. One of the team is appointed leader. They are then given a task, such as solving a financial or sales problem, installing a machine, or building a tower of toy bricks. At the end of the task all present are asked to say what the leader did or did not do to achieve the task, build the

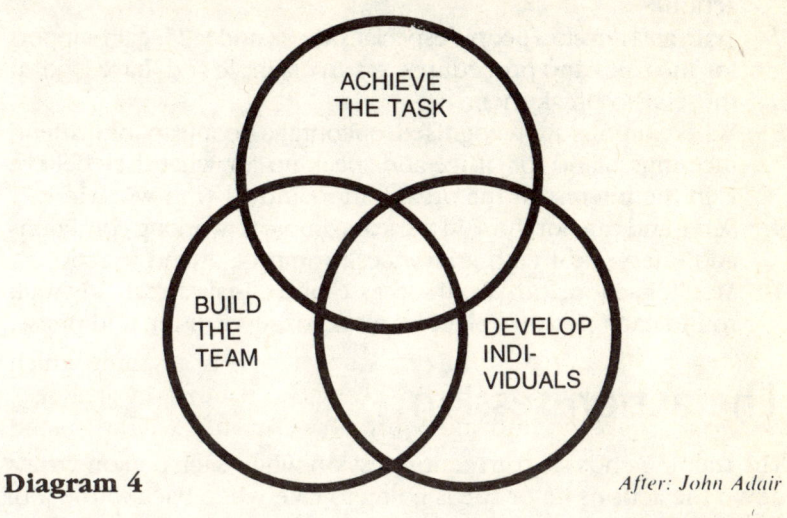

Diagram 4 *After: John Adair*

team and develop individuals. Any discussion on the qualities or the personality of the leader is banned. The exercises and discussions which follow can be repeated frequently with different people acting as the leader of the group.

Such training can be built into any existing managerial course. It is also necessary to include some of the more specific actions that the leader needs to take back on the job. These are listed below. All actions must be illustrated with a practical example relevant to the group. People learn from the particular to the general not vice versa.

The actions that need to be taught are:

1. Set the task of the team; put it across with enthusiasm and remind people of it often.
2. Make leaders accountable for four to fifteen people: practise and instruct them in the three circles.
3. Plan the work, check its progress, design jobs or arrange work to encourage the commitment of individuals and the team.
4. Set individual targets after consulting: discuss progress with each person regularly but at least once a year.

5   Delegate decisions to individuals. If not, consult those affected before you decide.
6   Communicate the importance of each person's job; support and explain decisions to help people apply them; brief the team together monthly on progress, policy, people and points for action.
7   Train and develop people especially those under 25; gain support for the rules and procedures, set an example and 'have a go' at those who break them.
8   Where unions are recognised, encourage people to join, attend meetings, stand for office and speak up for what they believe is in the interest of the organisation and all who work in it.
9   Serve and care for those in the team; improve working conditions and safety; deal with grievances promptly; attend functions.
10 Monitor action; learn from successes and mistakes; regularly walk round each person's place of work, observe, listen and praise.

The action session

The training ends with an action session when each person writes down the actions he or she is going to take when back in the job. The assessment of the training is not based on what those attending think of the speakers, or the visual aids, but on whether they are going to take any specific action in the particular area trained. If those being trained are not going to do anything about briefing for instance, then that part of the course was not effectively instructed. That is the crucial test.

The final stage of monitoring the instruction is to check six months later how many actions the trainees have carried out.

Course duration

All managers and supervisors need to receive between twelve and eighteen hours of instruction on how to get the best from people. It is more important to put everyone who leads through a short leadership course than to put a few on courses of much greater depth and length. At the highest level there may only be an appreciation course, but it is important that everyone should understand the common sense of the instruction being given.

Example
>After attending such a course a highly technical senior manager from the public service wrote: 'I now recognise that my whole understanding of management objectives was thoroughly vague before the course. To have a sympathetic approach to managing people (as opposed to the job) had never really occurred to me before.'

Group work

The effectiveness of management training courses depends on the maximum use of teams (five to eight people), where one of the team is appointed to act as leader to solve a particular problem and work out action. By this means courses of 24 or more can be run productively.

There are many forms of training which use team work. The method I am recommending here is based on discussing the actions of a leader in a task-centred framework. It is not concerned with sensitivity, or interpersonal relationships training and T Groups. There is clearly a place for such psychological activities (in the hands of clinically trained, qualified experts) dealing with people who are mentally disturbed. But as a means of leadership training for all managers and supervisors, such methods are unsuitable and unnecessary, and can make people worse leaders and have positively damaged others.

Experience at the bottom

If people are to spend much of their lives managing they should do a minimum of eighteen weeks in one job at the very bottom of the organisation, whether in the office or the factory. There is no other way of experiencing the need for leadership and at the same time realising the enormous potential that is there to be developed and involved.

Example
>A brilliant young man who had the academic world before him came into industry and was put to work in a paint store. After two months his store foreman told him that he was being

promoted from carrying half gallon cans to carrying one gallon cans. This decision after two months' repetitive work meant more to him than when he heard he had got a first class honours degree. It is only when you work at the bottom that you understand the importance of such simple things.

Development

The leader at each level must develop and select leaders. The best way of developing and judging people's leadership abilities is to give them practice in leadership. It is useful to:

- arrange for different people to act as holiday and other reliefs in the absence of the supervisor or more senior manager
- encourage the nomination of a person who 'acts in the absence of' (see Chapter 5)
- provide leadership opportunities (whether by leading in problem solving groups, working parties, or welfare activities such as pensioners' outings)
- encourage potential leaders to seek election as the shop steward or staff representative

If none of these are available then people should be encouraged to practise leadership activities in their spare time by leading local voluntary bodies, such as community service volunteers and youth clubs.

Selection

It is difficult to select as a possible leader someone who has not been observed in a leadership job. Therefore the development methods outlined also provide some evidence as to whether a person can, in practice, lead. As has been explained, one should not look for apparent qualities or styles. We must look for the person who in practice does the things an effective leader needs to do, and in his or her own way succeeds in achieving the task, building the team and developing individuals.

In the selection of leaders justice must be seen to be done: it is vital that more than one person should be involved in the selection process, and a panel can be useful. Although one or more people have the right of veto, the final selection should be left with the individual who is going to be directly accountable for getting the best out of that particular person.

Appointing leaders.

Leaders should be appointed by their senior manager; representatives should be elected.

There is real value in asking people at all levels, including the union, to recommend people who they believe would be good at leading. But on no account should they be elected into the executive leadership position. They must be appointed by the person to whom they are accountable.

Example

When crawling the face of a coal mine I asked the chargeman on the coal cutter how many people were absent from the shift on the previous Monday. There were quite a few. I asked him: 'Did you have a go at them on Tuesday for letting the team down?' 'No,' he said. 'I can't do that because I'm elected by them.'

There are two jobs – one to represent and one to make it happen. The second is the management leader and that person must be appointed not elected.

Women

Women comprise a considerable leadership resource, largely untapped. Much has been done to obtain equal pay, but the real problem is equal opportunity. Women frequently find themselves in factory jobs with male supervisors, or doing secretarial work for companies where there is no policy (or means) of promoting them to management level however good they are as leaders.

Many of us have daughters who are quite as competent as our sons in getting things done and organising people. But in industry and commerce we have not developed this resource. Some of the steps which need to be taken are:

- Evolving 'way through' jobs which women can move into. While

they are receiving any additional training they need they can prepare themselves for the first rungs on the leadership ladder
- Invite senior women who have 'made it' to talk to some of the younger women about how they have coped with career and family
- Send women on development courses, such as the Industrial Society's Pepperell Course, which show them what they can do themselves to develop as leaders
- Be flexible in employment policies for women. Special but regular hours may be needed at various points in their careers.
- Accept that on occasions their mobility may not be as great as a man's.

There is a need for some reverse discrimination not because of theories on 'women's lib' or equal opportunities but because it will pay organisations in the future to develop the potential of women.

7 TARGETS AND PERFORMANCE COACHING

If we are to give our best to our work each of us must know what we are responsible for, what is expected of us, how we are doing and how we can do better.

Example

Hundreds of women in a laboratory test were asked to work as hard as they could sorting blue from red balls on a tray for 20 minutes. Each one then rested and did the job again; but on the second occasion she had automatic counters which told her how many blue were going one way and how many red the other. In the second case where they could see how they were doing the women did 15-20 per cent more work.

For many years there was debate about the need for job descriptions. Mostly they were concerned with an employee's responsibilities and could become quite voluminous. They were often used negatively for purposes of hairsplitting about which job was whose, and defensively for a job holder to explain that some duty was not his or her responsibility because it wasn't down in the job description.

A much better idea was evolved 25 years ago: people started thinking not in terms of what they were responsible for but in terms of what they were paid to achieve. This was better expressed in the form of targets rather than job responsibilities. The trouble with this rather simple concept was that it fell into the hands of 'improvers' and 'experts', and soon there was a system developed which involved long term objectives, short term objectives, standards of performance, short term targets, key areas, and a number of other complications which became self-defeating.

The first thing to ensure is that everyone at every level has some simple targets to achieve. Each individual must know what these are and be seen regularly by their leader about their performance against these targets.

The simplest drill for target-setting is as follows.

Consult on targets

Individuals fill in a simple sheet showing:
- **(a)** what they think their main responsibilities should be, in five or six sentences.
- **(b)** five to seven targets which they think they can achieve by a definite date. Targets one and two may well be of the budgetary control type, eg the need to meet the agreed budget, or so much production at such-and-such a cost, or so many sales at such-and-such a price. The remaining targets cover other aspects of the job and will be personal to the job-holder. It may be to get a briefing system going within the next four months, or to try and improve the house-keeping, or develop a new product range, or improve quality standards by a stated amount by a particular time. These targets need to be as specific as possible, but they do not have to be expressed in financial terms. They may be better stated as actions most appropriate to the job, usually with a date for achieving them.

Set targets

Once the job-holder has written these suggested targets they should be discussed with the immediate boss. In the light of this discussion, the boss should make whatever changes in the targets he or she thinks right. The boss should consult before making this decision (see Chapter 9 on Decision-taking). The job-holder does not necessarily have to agree the targets, otherwise they will end up as a compromise. If the boss thinks people are either under or over-estimating what they can achieve, it is far better, after discussion, for the targets to be changed in line with what the boss believes is right. Leaders do not carry out manipulative discussions in which they try to get the person to say what they want to hear. Individuals have a duty to say what they think is right. The leader then has a duty after listening to say what is required. It might be necessary to insist on two or three things being achieved which the job-holder does not find particularly easy or attractive. Other aspects which are done perfectly well without targets can be left alone. The difference between job responsibilities and targets is that four people in an identical job will have identical job responsibilities, but their targets will be different and personal to each one of them. The target is concerned with the person giving of their best; and the best of each person differs. Furthermore, the particular thing that each person needs to concentrate on will differ from one to another.

Performance coaching

Having fixed the targets, job-holders should be seen every three, six or twelve months about their performance. This will not be assessed – as in the old days – on 'qualities' but on performance against set targets.

Example

Under the old staff assessment scheme, individuals would be sent for and told they had only been marked seven out of ten for initiative. People would then naturally ask if they could be given three examples of where they had failed to show initiative. At this point the interview usually came to a grinding halt because the interviewer could not provide these examples, but just knew that the person 'didn't have any initiative'.

Perhaps what is even worse than this is where people are not seen at all – comments on them are merely filed away. Clearly such schemes cannot improve performance at all. The performance interview should emphasise the action individuals should take to improve their performance. The nature of the interview is best described as performance coaching. An example of the most simple and basic policy issued by a major company is set out in Appendix 3.

Following the interview

The boss should make note of how well the targets were achieved, the job-holder's main strengths and any suggestions of what can be done to help that person further. This performance coaching form should preferably be read by the job-holder who should add any comments and sign it. Appendix 4 shows a simple example.

It is not expected that the job-holder will necessarily agree with what the boss has said. What matters is that the individual should *understand* what the boss has said and why it has been said. Thereafter the coaching form should go to the next level of management for countersigning.

Any comments on the person's potential and future development should be forwarded to the management development officer, if one exists, or to a higher level of management, so a record can be built up of the people of highest potential.

Development of high calibre people

People of high potential are one of the most valuable assets of the company. They are not just a departmental asset, although the boss of their current department is responsible for developing them to the full. Such high potential people should be known on a wide basis by other directors and departmental heads in the organisation.

Details of people of high potential should be recorded in a special folder. Names should be added to the folder whenever people display this high potential and equally removed from the list if they appear to have lost it. The system must allow for late as well as early developers. Apparent potential can change over the 40 years of a person's working life.

In large organisations photographs should be included with the person's details. This ensures that everyone knows who they are talking about.

Details of people held in this folder should be discussed at least once a year by the board, or most senior management. This helps to overcome the problem of senior managers being resistant to sparing one of their best people, or accepting an outstanding person from another department. If the people of highest potential are not widely known by the most senior management, there will be real problems in achieving the necessary movement. In the past too many managers have been caught by having a person recommended after the fashion of: 'I've got a very good person for you here; she's not much good in my department, but she'd do well in yours'. The regular annual discussion of people of high potential reminds all senior management of the importance of this crucial company asset and its full development.

8 Team briefing

If people are to be involved and able to participate in their work they must know what is happening and why. The reasons behind decisions are the motivators. People do not need to agree with decisions in order to co-operate, but they must know why. Profitability and efficiency do not depend upon obtaining obedience; but it is necessary to achieve people's co-operation. The difference between co-operation and obedience can be the difference between profit and loss. Communication, and in particular briefing, at every level, is the basis of real involvement. I cannot give my views or influence decisions in any way if I do not first understand what is going on around me at work and the reasons for it.

The cost of not commiunicating adequately can be seen in:

Misunderstandings

About half that goes wrong is due to people not understanding. The other half is due to various reasons including conflict. In one large company 18 out of the 35 stoppages in a five-year period were due to misunderstandings.

Failure to achieve commitment

Briefing will not make boring jobs interesting, but if people know why quality is so vital and are regularly reminded that their jobs matter, they will do them better.

Example
When a section of a company paid systematic attention to

briefing people each month about their work they reduced the total costs by six per cent and their processing costs by 20 per cent. This was because the 400 men concerned became more closely involved in the importance of what they were doing, how much they were achieving, and understood how each month they could better contribute to the success of the operation.

Failure to get people to co-operate with change

Organisations will only obtain the maximum benefit from change if people can be persuaded to co-operate with the new arrangements. People are naturally afraid of change, as it may adversely affect their own position and that of their colleagues. They need to be persuaded to co-operate with the changes.

Example
The repeated failure to achieve the claimed savings when introducing computers is not due to dishonest claims by the manufacturers nor to the incorrect design of hardware or software, but largely to the failure to achieve the co-operation of staff at all levels with the changes involved in making full use of the computer.

Increased productivity, which automatically involves change for people, depends on the ability to persuade individual employees to co-operate with that change. It is not enough to gain the agreement of full-time union officials or shop stewards. It is necessary to get the co-operation of each individual worker who has to change if 'extra productivity' is to have any practical meaning.

The 'them' and 'us' attitude

A major obstacle to co-operation is the 'them' and 'us' attitude, where everything is blamed on 'them'. This is largely a failure of communication, because people have not been told why something has been decided, only that 'they' have decided, or it is top policy. It becomes even more serious within the various levels of management where supervisors so often don't feel part of 'we', because they do not know the reasons behind the policies and decisions they have to pass on. Too often they find themselves having to say to their working group that something is being done because 'they' have decided it – because it is management policy. In organisations where supervisors are kept informed of the reasons behind decisions they are in a position to say 'we are doing this for the following reasons'. You cannot be 'we' unless you know 'why'.

The power of the grapevine to damage co-operation

The grapevine can be defined as the passing on of information by people who cannot be held accountable for what they say. The grapevine always works against co-operation because it denigrates the reasons behind decisions and plays on people's doubts and fears. It creates doubts about promotion policies and fears about people's future security.

Example

In an organisation where everyone was making a special effort to economise the grapevine spread the rumour that a new table had been bought for a director at a cost of £500. The grapevine talked of one rule for the rich and one for the poor. The truth was that the table had originally cost £500 but had been bought second-hand for a minimal sum.

Managements which try to make use of the grapevine are acting in ignorance of its powers of damage. Rumour will always circulate in large organisations, but the grapevine is less effective in doing damage in organisations which have adequate systems, for explaining to people the reasons behind decisions through their managers.

Methods of communication

The main methods of communicating to people what is happening and why are by the written word, at mass meetings, through elected representatives, face-to-face with individuals, or in small groups through the work-group leader at each level. All these methods have their place and are endorsed by the joint employer/trade union statement of 1980 as set out in Appendix 6. But the method which is most effective in achieving the high performance of people is to communicate through their boss in small groups on a regular basis. This system is known as Team Briefing.

The written word
Good for confirming facts, but not so effective in giving the reasons that persuade people to co-operate. Persuading people is best done by seeing them face-to-face.

Vital methods of written communication are notice boards, the managers' news sheet, the accountability chart and the employment handbook. The main drawback of the written word is that it cannot cope with questions and answers, and so often people understand only as a result of asking questions.

Representatives
Shop stewards and other elected representatives must be kept informed of management's views and the policies that affect them. But they should not be used as a main channel for passing these views on to their members. If shop stewards pass on the management reasons for a decision with enthusiasm they will be labelled as 'management men' and will not be re-elected. An equally serious drawback of using representatives as a main channel for briefing is they will take over the leadership of the group: the one who communicates is the one who leads.

The most important activity of a boss is to tell people what is happening, and why; people will turn to the person who knows. If the representative knows more about what is going on than the supervisor the representative will become the leader and influencer and not the supervisor. Management's ability to influence people on the factory floor in the UK has not been lost because of any deep seated plot. But in many cases, management has handed the job of telling people what is happening to shop stewards who, as a result, assume increasing control of employees.

Example

A great motor car company in New Zealand writes: 'We have now implemented Team Briefing with the foremen conducting their own sessions. They were so nervous at the prospect but are now full of confidence because of this new found ability to lead and manage. In Auckland, Team Briefing has been implemented, again with surprising results in terms of foremen assessment, increased communication and improved spirit within the workforce.'

This point is of particular importance when considering methods of participation. Most proposals are concerned with involving elected representatives in discussions at higher levels of management. This means representatives will become highly knowledgeable. It follows, therefore, that we will need to pay extra attention to keeping the middle managers and supervisors informed if they are to lead and if the representatives are to retain the confidence of those who elect them.

Example

A company developed a system where shop stewards were increasingly involved with management in decision-taking and were expected to take the resulting decisions back to the shop floor and explain them. Two years later none of the stewards were re-elected as they were looked on as bosses' men. Representatives are there to represent employees to management, supervisors are there to represent management to the employees.

Casual

Casual methods of communicating through management and supervisors do not work because:

- there are many levels
- people are busy and may be on shifts or away from base, eg drivers, sales teams or aircraft crews
- during periods of change when managers are likely to be busier than ever communication will decrease, at the very time it needs to increase
- it is time-consuming, since it takes longer to tell individuals than to tell people in small, organised groups

Explaining to individuals is less effective because it does not give people the opportunity to benefit from the questions and answers of others in the group.

Team Briefing

A leader will need to set up a simple checkable drill whereby explanations of relevant matters can be given to each working team at every level by the leader of that team on a regular basis.

This system of linked team meetings is known as Team Briefing. The five essential elements are:

- face-to-face explanation
- in teams
- by the leader who is accountable for the performance of the team
- regular and monitored
- on subjects relevant to achieving the highest performance from the team

How it works

The drill must:

1 Take place in teams

- between four and fifteen in each team briefing
- fewest possible number of steps between the top and bottom, ie a team briefing might consist of the manager, two assistant managers and the level below, so long as the number in the group is less than fifteen
- there must be no 'one-to-ones': where, for instance, there are supervisors or managers for each shift or heads of individual units (such as depots), such groups of managers and supervisors must be brought together by their common boss in a regular briefing, and not only dealt with individually
- where there is shift working all supervisors (whether on mornings, afternoons, nights or their rest day) must be brought together each month as a team with their manager

2 Involve the accountable boss

Briefing should be done by the immediate leader who is accountable for the work team at each level. Many managers say their foreman, chargehand or section leader in the office would be unable to brief adequately. Experience has shown that four out of five people are able to brief, and by so doing they become better team leaders.

Example

A chargehand in a food factory said she would rather talk to workers individually and couldn't really face talking to her whole team. I asked her if she could brief her team if her manager required her to do it. She asked if it would be like briefing the netball team. I said: 'Yes'. 'Oh', she said, 'that will be all right then because I do that every Saturday morning.'

Supervisors do not use the language of senior management when briefing. They talk in the language of their working group. As a result they are often rather better at putting the relevant thoughts and ideas across, and achieving the understanding and co-operation required. It is what people receive that matters, not what is transmitted.

3 Be regular and monitored

- Team Briefing should be held once a month or, if on the thirteen accountancy-period system, once each period. The credibility of the message depends on its regularity. At the bottom, a month is a long time between such meetings. Briefing may be required more often or in an emergency
- if there is a daily meeting for operational reasons it is worth extending one of these meetings each month for briefing. At management level the existing monthly meeting can be used for briefing
- a briefing meeting may last for 20-30 minutes: 20 minutes for explaining the points the leader wants to get over and the rest for any questions that the people present want to raise
- the regular team briefing at each level should be timed so that if there are any messages from the team briefing above they can be transmitted to the team below. At senior and other levels it will be necessary to put the times and dates of team briefings in diaries many months ahead
- time will need to be set aside for briefing. Normally the time can be found without any real disturbance of effective work, but there are cases of greater difficulty where companies take special steps: on continuous shift working, companies bring their afternoon

shift in early to be briefed or hold back the morning shift on overtime to staff the job, while the new shift is briefed by its supervisors in normal working time
- on batchwork, between loads or between periods of heavy pressure
- on transport, first thing in the morning or rostered for the weekend
- in shops, opening half an hour late or coming in half an hour early
- in offices, immediately after lunch
- on production lines, before starting up in the afternoon
- brief in a convenient place nearby in the office, works or mess rooms. Someone other than the briefer will need to answer the telephone
- briefers at every level will need a simple folder. For each briefing there will be a sheet showing date of briefing, time of starting and stopping, the subjects briefed and the names of anyone who was absent. There will be no typed minutes or agendas. One of the great shoe businesses requires a note of the meeting to be put in the production log – time it was held, how many present, subjects and questions asked
- like all effective systems Team Briefing will need to be checked by senior management. This is best done by looking at folders, or the log when 'walking the job', by sitting in on team briefings at a lower level, and by asking people why something is happening which was meant to have been briefed a few days before. If the answers are not known or are wrong those accountable for briefing can be asked to do it again. It is only when more senior managers show that team briefings are important enough to be checked that busy people make sure they are carried out

Example

Part of a large company had to make a major technical change which involved some redundancy – the alternative was to close the plant altogether. The change was explained to management, union representatives and then by each foreman to every person in every working group. At the meetings held by the union, everyone knew the union view and the management view. After discussion the workforce voted in favour of the union representatives negotiating the necessary technical changes. The foremen could only play this role because each month for the previous two years each foreman had held a team briefing on all subjects relevant to the team.

4 Cover relevant subjects

- progress: how is the team doing? Are we on budget or target? What have been the successes in the month? What have been the complaints and how can we handle them better? What did each member of the team achieve?
- people: who are the new appointments? What are the lateness or absence figures of the team? Changes in pay and promotion. Fears about people's security
- policies: some item which may have come right through the organisation, eg a pay settlement or a reorganisation which affects people in the team but where the decision may have been taken many levels higher
- points: items which leaders have noted down during the month to be stressed when they have the team together such as plans for the coming month

Example

During the month a mistake may have been made by one supervisor which the manager will deal with at the time, but will also note in the briefing folder. When all the supervisors are together, the manager can go over the point with them all, thus avoiding the mistake being made many times over.

- the subjects are those that affect the work of the members of the team. They usually arise from decisions or actions taken by the leader of the team or the leader's immediate boss. If there is anything relevant to be passed on from levels above, this will also be covered in the briefing. Where team briefings have not worked as well as they could it is because management has tried to use them primarily, if not exclusively, for passing messages from the top to the point of work. Since decisions which need to be briefed in this way do not occur at regular monthly intervals this makes a nonsense of Team Briefing
- to ensure local information is put over at each level, briefers at the level above should ask each leader what they are going to tell their team that month. They can then add to that local brief one or two points from above

- whenever anything is to be passed on note-taking is obligatory. The briefing folder is best used for this
- when something needs to be passed through three or more levels of management a brief setting out the main points should be provided. There should be space on this sheet so team leaders can quote examples which will best illustrate the point to their teams

Introducing Team Briefing

Companies which have successfully introduced Team Briefing have frequently taken the following steps:

- the senior line manager (managing director, general manager or unit manager) decides to introduce Team Briefing. The decision may be to introduce Team Briefing in one of the units as a trial and then to follow on with other units as experience is gained
- the senior manager should personally carry out monthly team briefings
- the senior manager should require all subordinate managers and supervisors to do likewise. It is like budgetary control; those of us who were required to do it developed the enthusiasm for doing it, not the other way round

Example

A newly appointed managing director of a great engineering company had to turn the company around urgently. One of his first actions in achieving success was to introduce Team Briefing of all 20,000 employees so that each individual understood his or her part in making the company successful. His method was to summon the top 150 directors and managers to hear a presentation and then told them that anyone who did not introduce Team Briefing within 23 months would find it a 'career limiting activity'!

- to be successful Team Briefing must be owned by the line management and not by training personnel or public relations
- all those briefing should receive at least one day's coaching in what to communicate and how to put it over. The Industrial Society can start the coaching and members of the company can

sit in and then carry it on. (See Appendix 5)
- to ensure the success of Team Briefing the chief executive and other managers must ask people what is being received on the factory and office floor when they are walking round the place of work. Managers at all levels should look in on Team Briefing lower down and see how it is going

9 Decision-taking

A crucial function of the leader is to take decisions. It is not just a question of getting the best decision but also taking it in a way which will obtain the best possible co-operation of the people who have to carry it out. Most decisions are not right or wrong but better or worse. An enthusiastically carried out worse decision may achieve better results than an unenthusiastically carried out better decision.

The most highly motivated decision is the one taken by the individual person. That person will often, by sheer effort, make the decision work even though it was not the best.

The problem, however, with the delegated decision is the difficulty of trusting the person to whom it is delegated to take the best one. Since the higher leader will always take the responsibility for any mistakes made, it is not easy to delegate the right to be wrong. Since trusting people involves risk-taking, it is necessary to discipline oneself into delegating decisions to individuals. And the more conscientious people are the more they will need self-discipline to make them delegate. A simple rule is that if the arguments for and against delegation of a particular decision are balanced, then delegate, but always to a particular individual who can be held accountable.

Decisions for groups

Where a decision is needed which affects a group the decision should be taken by the leader of that group. It should not be delegated to the group as a whole. Group decisions are likely to be on the basis of the consensus, which means either a compromise or the majority overcoming the minority. Frequently, neither of these methods produces the best decisions, nor can anyone be held accountable, nor are they decisions which obtain the enthusiasm of the people in the group. The people who did not agree with the decision feel they are being voted down by the majority or manipulated into going along with something that they consider a mistake.

A decision affecting the whole group cannot please every member of the group. The question, therefore, is how to get the greatest enthusiasm behind the decision. It is fashionable to consider the so-called consensus decision as the best way of doing it. Reality shows this to be untrue. People on the whole prefer a situation where the leader takes the decision after the fullest consultation with the group. The leader does not try interminably to achieve unanimity where it does not exist but, after consultation, announces the decision and the reasons behind it, and calls for co-operation to carry it out. Most people are able to give enthusiasm to decisions arrived at in this way because they feel they have had their say, and it is one of the jobs of the leader to take the ultimate decision.

Individual accountability for decisions is important, so a check can be made later to see who was the person who took the better or less good decision. It can be argued that those who take better decisions are lucky. There is much more in it than luck, and it has been rightly said that it is good policy to promote leaders who appear to be lucky in their decisions!

The method

A simple drill of decision-taking can be built round the words consider, consult, crunch, communicate and check.

1 Consider

What is the decision to be taken, does it need taking, by when and by whom should it be taken? Who is the individual nearest the point of action to whom the decision could be delegated?

In deciding when to take the decision do not take it earlier than is necessary, but it may be worth remembering the number of people throughout the organisation who may be in neutral waiting for the decision to be taken. If there is delay people should be told when a decision can be expected. The market and much else cannot wait for the perfect decision.

2 Consult

Collect all available information but do not amass more than you can cope with. There is a grave danger of paralysis by analysis.

Consult all those affected and those who can contribute to the decision, including union representatives and consultative committees.

There is no such thing as the prerogative of management not to consult those affected before a decision is taken. To talk in this way is to suggest management has the prerogative to be stupid. The only exception to the rule of consultation before decision is where time does not permit consultation to take place.

Example

> If you see a man putting his hand under a moving knife you do not consult him before you knock his hand away. If you consulted first, he might admire your motivational thoughts, but would have preferred to have kept his hand.

To give of our best we do not have to agree with the decisions that have been taken at a higher level. But what drives us mad is when we are not consulted about something in which we are deeply involved before the decision was taken, nor even told afterwards the reasons why.

3 Crunch

If a decision is to be taken the most important single point is that it should be taken. There will not be a perfect answer but it is always possible to take the least worst.

When taking the decision the leader will not necessarily do what those consulted think best. Consultation is not compromise. It is the activity of one party sincerely seeking the views of another before a decision is taken. The leader has wider responsibilities than those being consulted. After listening to the views of members of the group the leader must fit them into any wider considerations such as achieving the budget, relations with other departments, and his or her longer experience, vision and judgement, and then decide what is best.

When the moment of decision comes, however, there is real value in the old idea of sleeping on it first. This old procedure appears to allow the sub-conscious mind to sort out the weighting of the various factors. It prevents the appalling dangers of counting the arguments for and those against and deciding the question on the quantitative basis of the greatest number of arguments. There are frequently ten reasons for not doing something but only one for doing it. Qualitatively, however, the one for doing it may be of a totally different order to the ten against.

Example
On looking back on what I consider to have been one of the most important decisions of my life, I recall asking the advice of one of the wisest directors of ICI about whether I should leave the company and come to The Industrial Society. He told me that he would not tell me what to decide but how to decide it. He said:

(a) Decide on which day the answer must be given.
(b) Work back four days from that date which in his view should include a Sunday.
(c) Up to that four days collect all the information possible about the new job, about prospects in the existing job, consult and seek advice, and finally write out all the arguments, for and against, on a piece of paper.
(d) Then destroy the paper. Whenever the subject comes into your mind during the ensuing four days, reject it.
(e) On the final day wait until the subject first arises in your mind and then decide to do what seems to be right.

In the event the arguments when analysed were stacked 10:1 against taking the new job. However, on the final day it seemed right to come to the Society. Now 24 years after the event it is possible to analyse in detail why that decision was correct whereas few of the now apparent factors could have been discerned, or were indeed in existence, at the time the decision was taken.

This form of decision-taking steers nicely between the laziness of not doing the analysis and the arrogance of insisting that inspiration does not exist.

4 Communicate
Brief to all those affected the decision that has been taken and the reasons behind it. Having consulted earlier it will be possible to try

and answer some of the points that were made to help people live with the decision that has been taken and carry it out with enthusiasm. Now that the decision has been taken all leaders at every level must put the decision over with all the enthusiasm they can muster, whether they agree with the decision or not.

This point is widely misunderstood today where there are too many cases of professional people in industry and in education, refusing to support decisions from above with which they disagree. 'Don't blame me for this decision, it's them up there who decided.'

This approach is one cause of the 'them and us'. It leads to frustration of the individual who has to carry out the decision, but no one feels it their responsibility to explain the policy and help them live with it.

If a person feels the decision is so bad they cannot put it over then that person has no alternative but to resign with all that implies.

5 Check

The last step in decision-taking is some system of grievance, whereby a decision can later be challenged by those affected if people consider a serious mistake has been made. It is better to have a system where the odd wrong decision can be put right, than a system where there is endless argument and discussion designed to avoid wrong decisions – with the result that many decisions are taken too late, and some not at all.

Until such time as the grievance procedure has worked (see Chapter 15, Trade unions) the decision stands. There is nothing in a grievance procedure which diminishes the authority of the leader. Leaders who can admit they were wrong and change their decision in the light of new evidence will increase their authority as leaders, not diminish it.

Check that the decision was carried out. We can use the simplest kind of checking or monitoring – perhaps the best way is to go and see for ourselves. 'Walking the job' is crucial in this respect.

Check how the decision turned out. Learn by successes and failures and note who seems to take the more successful decisions.

The whole form of commonsense decision-taking outlined in this chapter runs quite counter to the much advocated, and recently fashionable concept of a 'decision-taking spectrum'. This advocates that on some matters one should take an authoritative decision and give an order, whereas on others, at the other participative end of the 'spectrum', one should delegate the decision to the group and let them decide by consensus.

The idea of changing one's style of decision-taking, depending on the occasion, goes totally against an important ingredient of leadership: that people should know they have a reasonably consistent boss. They should understand the way the boss goes about things, for better or worse, instead of wondering whether they are being manipulated or being given a straightforward instruction.

Decision-taking policy

There is much confusion over decision-taking, especially when so much attention is given to participation, that companies have found it valuable to define their decision-taking philosophy – an example is given in Appendix 8.

10 Discipline

Where people live or work together in a community there must be rules of behaviour. One of the required activities of a leader is to get people to co-operate with these rules. This is the meaning of discipline.

Discipline is not a polite word for punishment. Discipline is much wider than punishment. Only in a few cases and as a last resort is some form of sanction needed. Managers are too inclined to argue that if we cannot punish a person we cannot do anything about getting that person to keep the rules. There is an even stranger concept that if we cannot sack people we cannot be expected to get their co-operation. Of course we can!

An example of this unrealistic outlook is to be seen in the way so many people deal with sickness absence. The argument goes that you can do nothing to discourage people from taking advantage of sickness absence schemes, because you cannot, in practice, challenge a medical certificate, or punish anyone for taking advantage of the system. Effective leaders have always recognised that it was part of their job to encourage people in the team not to take time off unnecessarily. Leaders do this by having it out with anyone they feel is taking an unfair advantage of the situation. Of course where people are seriously ill, effective leaders will do all they can to encourage them to stay away. But serious illness is not the main reason for absence from work.

For the most part, discipline is a question of getting people to come in on time, work safely, pay attention to quality and good housekeeping, not to smoke in the wrong place, to work a full day and carry out the procedures. The first thing is to see that people know what the rules are; this requires a written staff handbook setting out the basic rules.

People will co-operate better with rules if they know the reasons for them. In some company handbooks the rule is printed in black on one page and the reasons for the rule are printed on the opposite page or below in red.

Thereafter, it is the responsibility of immediate leaders to see that the people for whom they are responsible understand the rules and carry them out. Involving the immediate leader who works among the group and can influence them from day-to-day is the best way to get people to co-operate with the rules.

Example

In a very hot manufacturing unit it was normal during a heatwave for people on the 2.00 pm – 10.00 pm shift to give up and go home at 4.00 pm. A young foreman was determined to meet this challenge, but having jollied his shift along from Monday to Thursday was told by the shop steward that they were going out at 6.00 pm on the Friday. He spoke to the 36 men in the group on the grass outside the building from 5.45 pm until 6.00 pm and, on his own authority, guaranteed their wages for this period. As a result of persuading them to see their duty they went back to work.

Later the shop steward told the young foreman that he, the shop steward, could not have said those things to the men because if he had he would have been labelled a management man – but of course the foreman was meant to be a management man. Other managers also commented that they had not realised a foreman could stop an unofficial strike in this way. They thought it was a matter for the industrial relations department and the disputes and discipline machinery.

Where people break the rules, they should be seen by their immediate boss. If more serious action is needed, then the case should be referred to a higher level of management on the immediate boss's recommendation.

Where punishment or sanctions are needed, a clear drill should be laid down. (It is worth remembering that modern industry has greater powers of punishment than the armed forces. In the armed services, you could put a man in detention but you couldn't normally deprive him of his livelihood – in industry and commerce we can.)

1 These drills should not permit an immediate boss to dismiss

anyone without it being referred to a higher level for the case to be carefully considered. However, the immediate boss should be able to suspend the person on full pay until the case is heard.
2 The exception to this is where individuals in their first three months have shown they are not right for the job, and there has been a failure in selection. This form of dismissal is known in some companies as 'de-selection', but should only be applied in the first three months of a person's employment. Thereafter, to remove a person's livelihood is a more serious decision than declaring a piece of machinery or an office system obsolete, and should be handled with at least the same seriousness.
3 It will be necessary to have warnings in writing on the person's file.
4 Where representative bodies exist the individual should always have the right to be accompanied by the appropriate representative. Where dismissal is a possibility, the representative should be informed and may well be present at the time the case is heard and the decision given.

The law gives protection against unfair dismissal to employees with certain specified service. If challenged it is for the employer to prove that dismissal was justified. For this purpose, organisations need to carry out the above drills as a minimum.

Whenever some form of sanction is needed it is important to go for justice in each case, rather than a policy which, under the heading of 'fairness-for-all', can so often become a policy of 'equal-misery-for-all'.

Example

A young laboratory assistant found smoking on a non-smoking chemical plant was dismissed. Some months later an older chargehand was found smoking on the same plant and was also dismissed on the grounds that the punishment must be the same. Punishment meted out to the chargehand was in fact infinitely greater, in that he could never again get a job of similar level; whereas the lab assistant could go round the corner and do just as well next door.

If punishments are different, however, the grapevine will give some cynical explanation. It is important for the leader to explain that what appears on the surface to be unequal treatment is in fact a serious effort to achieve equal justice.

Where people ask for an exceptional concession on some special occasion, again the argument often goes: If you can't give it to all you can't give it to one.

The effective leader will, however, continually struggle to do justice by individuals, even though, on the face of it, this may seem unfair between one person and another. If, however, leaders explain what they are doing and why they are doing it, the team will achieve more than if the leader dealt with people on a totally uniform basis.

Example

A staff grade scheme had as one of its general principles that a man might have up to three days off if his wife was seriously ill and he could not get help to look after the children.

A case arose where a man who had never taken advantage of this in twelve years needed six days before he could get help for his children. This was refused him, whereas another man who took advantage of the three-day role at least three times a year continued to get his three days whenever he asked for them.

This is an example of applying discipline solely by rule of book. That kind of inflexibility is better practised by a machine than by people. It has little to do with leadership or justice. To allow a flexible system to operate without abuse it is important to have a union which can question a decision if they think something improper has taken place.

The law

As a result of recent legislation a written disciplinary procedure is essential, as is a proper system of written warnings to people.

It is necessary in any disciplinary procedure to make it clear that there are certain offences which will incur summary or immediate dismissal. However, the wording of such a clause or published document should clearly state that before dismissal of any kind takes place the case will be heard in a calm atmosphere. No one has the right to summarily dismiss anyone until this procedure is carried out. In such cases of serious apparent offences the leader has the duty to summarily suspend a person on full pay until the case is heard. Someone who arrives drunk on the plant or appears to have stolen some item should be sent home until the case is heard.

Unions and management, however, recognise that by the sincere effort to codify so much in law there is a tendency for employees to be treated as legal notions rather than as flexible individuals.

Of course the law must be kept and upheld, but those responsible for others must not allow the fear of the law to remove their humanity. If, therefore, leaders, in an effort to be realistically human, break the letter of the law by mistake they should remember that tribunals and the like are most understanding in these matters. Further, it is not the end of the world if, in these sincere circumstances, a fine has to be paid.

11 Walking the job

A vital activity for leaders is to walk regularly round the place of work of those in the enterprise, department or section. Not only does it help to lessen the 'us' and 'them' attitude; it is a good way of keeping in touch with what is really happening and it answers such questions as – Are decisions being carried out? Do people understand why?

Many managers have become too busy to carry this out and various forms of technological equipment have made them think they are in touch when in fact they are not.

Example

A lathe operator in a factory near Leeds pointed out that in the past although the boss of the firm might have been thought to be an arrogant so-and-so, it was 'much more human in those days'. When asked why, he said: 'He was in front of my machine at twenty to nine every day. Now we never see them, they are so busy talking to each other, attending meetings, looking at paper plans.'

Regularity

It is necessary in these busy days to mark off in the diary the time to walk round the place of work. Senior people with many responsibilities may need to ask their secretaries to ensure all departments are periodically covered; the need for such a systematic approach is even more important for managers who find this kind of thing difficult.

Subjects of discussion

The object is to observe, listen and periodically praise. It is not to correct people except through the line of leadership, that is to say, going to the foreman or team leader, and asking why something is happening. When talking to an individual it seems best usually to talk about the job; the job and the work is the great link between people.

Monitoring

Walking the job is a prime means of checking on what the situation really is. Examples are visiting customers with sales representatives, discussing experiments in research departments, looking at operating figures displayed on wall charts in offices, reading letters which are being typed – there is a great art in knowing where to look.

Example

A great retailing managing director went to visit a food factory to see if it was suitable for supplying his chain stores. When he arrived and was received, instead of walking round the factory he walked round the perimeter fence. As he left he said he would 'come back again when the factory had good housekeeping and hadn't had to be specially cleaned up for his visit.' By walking outside the factory he had seen all the things that had obviously been cleared out for his visit!

Accompanied or alone

Visits should be entirely informal and unannounced. Good manners demand that one should put one's head into the boss's office first in case he or she would like to come round at the same time. Great trains of intermediate officials should be discouraged.

Praise

It is important to discipline oneself to give praise. It is too easy to see what is wrong, rather than what is right. If it has not been normal for managers to walk round the place of work, there will be those who resent it as showing lack of trust. It is only by seeing us regularly that people will realise we come because it is part of the job and we actually care about what is happening.

12 Job design

Although many jobs are repetitive and at times tedious, effective leaders can arrange them in a way which makes them less bad, if not particularly satisfying. Jobs can also be organised so people feel a greater sense of participation in producing an end product.

Job rotation

In years gone by a good deal was done on job rotation, in which each person in the team would move round. Such rotation is resisted by people who want to settle down to one particular job. In effective organisations work group leaders do get members of the team to do one another's jobs because it increases flexibility and provides cover during absence. However, job rotation will only increase involvement marginally, because it means doing a succession of jobs, each equally repetitive.

Longer job cycles

A better solution is to organise the operation so that each operator has a number of different things to do.

Example

A vacuum cleaner was originally constructed by operators on a production line carrying out short cycle jobs – such as one operator repeatedly putting a nut on a bolt of each sweeper as it passed by.

When the same company came to make a floor polisher, the operator sat at a bench and trays of the various parts making up the polisher revolved round. Each operator was therefore able to build up a complete polisher step by step and put their number on it. The repetition was a longer cycle and the individual could take some pride in the end product.

The second way of organising the job was a good deal less boring than the first.

Group technology

Here, jobs are put together so teams carry out a whole process rather than the product going to a number of different specialist departments.

Job enrichment

The fourth, and even better way of making jobs more worthwhile is to enrich the depth of the job. Individuals are encouraged to take decisions about how they will do their job. They are involved in discussions before the leader takes a decision on behalf of the group and they inspect the job themselves rather than it being done by an inspector.

Example
In an aircraft engine repair unit, the supervisor of each small team was trained and qualified as an inspector and carried out the inspection of his own team's production. This runs quite counter to the normal method of setting up a separate inspection department and may seem impractical. It is worth noting therefore, that in this particular case the inspection was to AID standards and was as searching as any.

Leaders who delegate much of their job to a secretary and let her get on with it, rather than using her as a dictating machine or a copy typist, will not only get through a great deal more work, they will make the secretary's job more worthwhile.

This form of job enrichment is achieved largely by delegating many of the decisions about the job to a lower level. Jobs are more worthwhile if people are able to take their own decisions and are accountable for the results (see Decision-taking, Chapter 9). It is more effective to feed control data to individuals so they can take the necessary action, rather than to an individual's boss who will 'correct' them.

Profit centres

At higher levels jobs are made more worthwhile and rewarding by organising them on a profit-centred basis rather than a functional one. Jobs will be more rewarding, more fun and less frustrating where a unit is producing, maintaining and selling the product than where specialist service units take over these activities for an organisation as a whole.

In deciding how far to go towards more realistic job structuring, one will take into account that specialisation and the functional approach may often appear on paper to show savings. However, these savings may be illusory. Greater savings are achieved by getting people to work to their highest performance, through making individuals accountable, giving them satisfaction and allowing them to see demonstrable achievement.

13 Relevant conditions of employment

Chapter 4 made it clear that in achieving high performance the most important factor is the action the work group leader takes. However, the conditions of employment – that is to say the way people are paid, their physical working conditions and the arrangements which give them a sense of security – can either help the leader's actions or work against them.

Example

If an organisation is trying to cut overtime it is unwise to have foremen paid overtime money. The foreman can clearly influence the amount of overtime worked, but if by so doing he knows his own money in the following week or month is going to be cut, the conditions of employment are working against management's objectives.

It is wiser therefore to put the foreman on a payment scheme whereby more senior management assesses what a reasonable amount of overtime would have been, and then spreads the payments over a three-monthly period.

In deciding on relevant conditions of employment it is necessary to ask what people need (and this may sometimes be different from what people want) if they are to give of their best to their work.

Pay – wages

Piecework, bonus and commission schemes are inclined to act as fining schemes once they have been applied for any length of time. A person will quickly earn up to the level they can and then the fear is that the money will be cut back. The individual will therefore take defensive action to prevent this happening by refusing new jobs or work of high quality. Another widely used defensive method is to work below capacity so that if a difficult piece of work has to be done it is possible to keep one's money stable by working at full capacity for a short period. People today cannot afford fluctuating money. Regular money is needed for housing, premiums, hire-purchase and holidays.

A more effective method of payment is based on evaluating the work of one job against another (job evaluation). Higher performance in a particular job will be rewarded but the payment scheme will not include any arithmetical arrangements which automatically cut back on pay if performance declines. If a person's performance falls below the level for which they are being paid the immediate leader sees the person to find out why. Only if, after warnings, the performance continues to be unsatisfactory is the person (with due notice) demoted to a lower level of payment.

However hard you try it is always difficult to achieve justice between one job and another and between jobs with different levels of loading – particularly as, in some cases, the work load will simply not be there for the person to do. A helpful principle in such cases is that people will work more readily if they receive the same amount of pay for unequal work than if they receive different levels of pay for the same amount of work. The first situation seems to be regarded as the luck of the draw or the 'rub of the green', but the second as rank injustice.

Example

>In a set of unofficial strikes the disrupters succeeded finally in getting the men out because they could demonstrate that regular employees were receiving less than half the money that self-employed men on the same sites were being paid for the same amount of work.

Very low wages are counter-productive. If more money can be obtained by being at home then people are not being paid enough at work. Efficiency and profitability depend on high performance. Low pay with low performance is uneconomic.

Pay – salaries

On the salary side the danger is not that pay is too tightly tied up with a person's hour-to-hour performance, but rather that there is not a firm enough relationship between performance and salary increases. This often comes about because salary revision is carried out at far too high a level in the organisation, with the result that the directors who know the salary policy don't know the individual's performance, and the supervisor who knows the performance is not involved in the application of the salary policy. It is worth noting therefore the companies who use salary cards rather than salary lists, and distribute each person's card to the immediate boss who can pencil in a recommended salary increase under the general guidance of the salary policy. The recommendations can then be amended if necessary by the next level up, and so on through the structure.

When the time comes for informing the person about salary increase it is done by the immediate leader together perhaps with the next up. They can then talk in some detail about the individual's performance and how both performance and salary can be improved.

Acceptance of change

It is difficult to get people to co-operate with change, with all the associated fears. But change is made more acceptable by protecting people as far as possible from its monetary cost. Effective leaders will therefore, wherever possible, keep people on their present salary or level of pay even if they are to be moved into other jobs with less responsibility. It will pay a leader to use general buy-outs in getting rid of some restrictive practice or irrelevant payment scheme. Those companies who go in for generous redundancy policies not only achieve the first de-manning but make any subsequent de-manning easier. Long warnings of change also bring security. To get rid of people at a moment's notice may appear to have advantages, but it is worth remembering that whenever you treat people in this way you put everyone remaining in the company on a moment's notice as well. People will then naturally devote themselves to protecting their own security rather than getting on with the job and giving of their best.

Physical working conditions

In thinking about the design of restaurants, or how people are seated in offices, the key factor is the relevance of the conditions to high performance. Does putting people together in one canteen improve communication by enabling departments, and people at various levels within departments, to sit and eat together and to participate in discussion? It is argued that if there is one canteen people still sit at different tables depending on their level in the company. The fact, however, is that many companies go in for single status eating and seem to get results in terms of an improvement in attitude and a lessening of the 'them' and 'us'. In providing recreation it may be much wiser to have on the site a bar in a rickety hut, which opens at the end of a working day, than to have a plush recreation club miles away.

When seating people in offices what matters is not an impressive flow diagram for the paper work, or whether the vista planning is attractive to architects, but how people can be arranged in small teams where a leader can build up the necessary 'team keenness', where people will not feel like cogs in the wheel or exhibits in a showcase. A rule of thumb is to arrange screens and partitions so that no more than twelve people sit within sight of each other. Within their own area let individuals arrange themselves as they like. Wherever possible, set the individual free.

Single status

Underlying all conditions of employment is the great divide between the treatment of office staff and factory workers. Employment conditions for office workers are built on the principle that it is best to trust people, whereas conditions for factory workers are built on the basis that people cannot be trusted. Hence the need for time-clocks, reduced wages for sickness absence and pay measured by hourly results.

These two very different sets of conditions may have been explicable many years ago when the office and shop floor worker came from different educational backgrounds. But today it is impossible to justify the disparity – as, for example, when a brother will go on to the shop floor and his sister, of identical background, will go into the office.

More serious is that people in non-trust conditions are discouraged from becoming trustworthy.

There is one exception to the policy of harmonisation of conditions. If by putting section leaders or chargehands on shift conditions they are prevented from working alongside their team and using the tools, the lesser evil is to keep them on payroll conditions yet still require them to carry out the management leadership job.

In all other cases management need to introduce a common ladder of conditions for office and shop floor. When new technological jobs arise in the factory the relevant conditions are likely to be those of the staff and not of the payroll. People doing jobs such as operating control panels and inspection, jobs which require reliable and responsible action, are better motivated by staff conditions.

Every opportunity should thereafter be taken to transfer more and more jobs to staff conditions. In the case of those companies who have the good fortune to set up on new sites, it is best to start with one set of conditions from the beginning.

Hours

It is dangerous to let overtime hours get out of hand as it affects the leader's ability to achieve people's co-operation. There is no harm in people working 35-45 hours each week, but more than 60 is unwise. Of course people want the overtime money, but a leader must think about what is relevant to high performance. The more flexible hours can be around people's needs the better. For example, there are great human resources available in young women, who often must see their children off to school at around 9 am and be home by 4 pm. Between these hours they have much dedicated service to offer.

There are doubts about whether it is realistic for both the individual and the organisation to give daily flexibility to start and finish times. Where it can be arranged it works well for some people to start at 9.30 am and work later, but this needs to be a regular routine. The concept that anyone can come in at any time up to a 'core' time of say, 10.30 am, does not seem appropriate.

Although it is fashionable, there are very grave doubts about re-introducing time clocks for staff even though they may record over a week or a month. Time recording devices of any sort concentrate people's minds on being paid for time in attendance instead of being paid for their contribution to the job. Clocks are also inclined to lessen a leader's first task, which is to see that people are there and have plenty to do.

Special grants

In spite of improved Government welfare services, people can still run into financial hardship. It will benefit a company enormously to have a special fund with which to help employees. The key to such a fund is that all those who lead should know of its existence and be on the watch for people who are in trouble. If this is not done the really worthy case never comes to the company's attention because the individual concerned will not ask.

14 Participative machinery

If the most effective decisions are to be taken and carried through with enthusiasm, those who take the decisions must be aware of the factors involved and the possibilities available. One part of this is to obtain the views and ideas of those who will have to carry out the decisions. This process of upward communication and participation is concerned not only with the decision-taker being aware of the facts but with the situation being made vivid for the people at the bottom.

Example

All who have worked in organisations of any size will know how difficult it is for people at the bottom to effect decisions which have been taken at a higher level: whether it is supplying more telephone lines or removing a redundant machine from the factory floor.

So often it is only when the representative in a participative committee explains the situation that the necessary action is taken.

There are various ways of keeping in touch with what is happening at the point where the products are made on the factory floor, or where they are sold at the counter. Casual methods for keeping in touch will not be adequate in organisations of 50 or more people.

Management responsibility

Managers and supervisors at all levels should have written into their responsibilities the need to pass the views of their staff upwards. However, this method will not be adequate on its own in organisations with three levels of management or more. By the time each level has reported the views of the level below the facts may get through but the vividness of the message will be lost. Furthermore, if junior managers repeatedly take the interests of their team to the level above, there comes a time when the senior manager will suspect the problem lies in the leader's management, not the team.

There is every evidence that the feedback involved in upward communication requires a different mechanism from the one for downward communication – every engineer knows you cannot have a feedback mechanism running on the prime mover: to find out what speed a car is doing it is necessary to have a speedometer directly connected to the wheels.

Walking the job

Managers have always been more effective where they have walked round regularly talking to people about their jobs, finding out the problems and the ideas of the individual doing the job. It may be by visiting customers with their staff, serving on a counter, spending time down in a machine shop or with a pilot in the aircraft. It is not for senior leaders to take decisions at these levels, for if they do they will cut the ground from under intermediate bosses. They are walking round primarily to find out what is happening in practice by observing and asking questions.

Example

A shipyard appeared surprised that it was in serious financial troubles. If the most senior managers had spent less of their time studying historical figures in the office and more time walking the job and seeing with their own eyes the low level of activity, they might have been able to take action in time to avert disaster.

Although walking the job is vital it will not be adequate on its own. People will not normally communicate bad news about their work to a very senior manager who is bothering to talk to them. They will not pass on the real problem, which may be that the foreman is not adequate, that the equipment is defective or that there is a shortage of telephone lines. Nor can they be counted upon in this situation to mention their ideas on how the job can be done better.

Suggestion schemes

Suggestion schemes are a valuable method of carrying people's ideas up to the level where a decision can be taken to incorporate them. The key to the success of such schemes lies with junior managers. They should encourage their people to make suggestions through the schemes and then publicise those ideas which have been accepted. The rewards do not need to be especially large. Suggestion schemes, however, have to rely on the written word. They do not produce the valuable cross-fertilisation of ideas which takes place in a small consultative group where members are putting forward suggestions and progressively improving each other's ideas.

Attitude surveys

The views of various people in the organisation can be gauged by attitude surveys. Here the design of the questionnaire is important, as the wording can affect the answers.

Example

A company surveying attitudes to trade unions asked whether the staff would like their salaries settled by 'collective bargaining'. Most of the staff said 'No'.

Had the question been whether staff would support management/staff unions 'negotiations' on salary bands the answer would have been significantly different.

The words 'collective bargaining' were loaded in the eyes of the staff concerned.

The attitude survey has the advantage, like a referendum, of gauging the number of people holding a particular view. But, as with referendums, it is most unwise to allow them to dictate the decisions. Deciding the right course of action in the long-term interest of the company and the people in it is the responsibility of management.

Similarly, the attitude survey, which must end up as a written report for the decision-takers, never achieves the vividness of a meeting between the decision-taker and representatives of the people concerned.

Consultative efficiency committees

The most effective way of transmitting people's ideas and attitudes to decision-taking level is through such committees. Many companies have committees in which employee representatives meet with the most senior management to discuss progress and future plans. Some of these committees, whether they are called works committees or joint consultation committees, have a history of more than 70 years in this country. Some have found they have concentrated too much on eating and washing facilities. Too many have been used for exhorting representatives rather than for sincerely seeking their views before decisions are taken. It is claimed that some of these committees have been used to discourage the growth of trade unionism. Consultative efficiency committees are not for these purposes. They can serve the interest of the company and the employees most productively if the committees have the following characteristics:

Size
A committee should consist of not more than fourteen people, comprising three or four management appointees, while the remainder will be elected representatives.

Departmental
It has been found that if the consultative committee covers too wide a range of interests with, for example, representatives from accounts, research, transport, manufacture, the tool room, different sales departments, etc, the subjects in common among those representatives will tend to be limited to canteens, lavatories and so forth.

If, on the other hand, there is a research department consultative committee, or a tool room consultative committee (ie they are departmental) representatives will have something really worthwhile to contribute on how research work can be better organised and better facilities made available. There may then need to be a linking company consultative committee, which can meet at less frequent intervals.

Purpose
The purpose of the committee is to seek sincerely the views of those

present, before decisions are taken.

The subjects can be anything and everything to which those round the table can usefully contribute information, views and knowledge. Seventy per cent of the discussion ought normally to be about subjects which the senior manager has put on the agenda to find out what people think before taking a decision. It is useful to have one major subject for discussion at each meeting, and representatives should be warned of this subject at their previous meeting so they have time to prepare their views and collect the ideas of their constituents. Such subjects might include:

- improving the selection and training of supervisors
- providing more mechanical aids to achieve efficiency
- the effect on efficiency of various types of open-plan or small-team offices
- new plans for developing the area or business
- ways of organising work and altering hours

The consultative committee is not there for explanation and briefing. This is the job of Team Briefing (see Chapter 8). Nor should it be used for negotiation, ie joint agreement on decisions. Consultation and negotiation may at times become very close, but the effective chairman will remind the committee of its purpose, and where negotiating bodies are recognised, negotiation should take place through a separate part of the machinery. Where consultation and negotiation are muddled together chaos can result. Management will tend to discourage subjects for consultation in case they should be forced into negotiating a decision with which they do not agree, but for which they will be accountable. The atmosphere of consultation, where everybody contributes, is different from that of negotiation where the cards are frequently played close to the chest.

Example

A company negotiating and discussing how oil tankers might be driven for distances under a productivity bargain, discussed in detail the new stopping points, crew changeover procedures, details of parking and the like. After two days it was finally accepted that the extended route to the new stopping point could be undertaken for an additional 20p an hour.

As the discussion broke up the trade union side said 'And

what is more, for another 5p we will drive another 40 miles', with the result that the whole detailed discussion was totally wasted.

This occurs where consultation and negotation are merged into one.

It is more productive to discuss first of all, how the cake can be made bigger – how people can contribute more effectively without being expected to do anything unreasonable. Thereafter negotiations should take place on how much needs to be paid in sharing out the extra cake, before it is agreed the action should be taken.

Representatives

The management representatives should include the head of the unit who should act as chairman, ie the departmental head for a departmental committee. It is that person who is discussing with representatives how the department can be more effective and how jobs can be made more worthwhile for people.

There should always be a first line supervisor sitting as one of the three or four management representatives.

The elected representatives should include the union representatives, where unions exist. For many years companies used to consult with works councillors who were not recognised by the trade unions, but negotiate with shop stewards. Not surprisingly, this did not produce the best results. Organisations have found that although it is not effective to consult and negotiate at the same time, it is important that the people with whom one negotiates the share of the cake should also participate in how to make bigger cakes. When people find how difficult it is to make anything at all, it rubs off on what they consider to be fair demands for more. Also, it prevents unending demarcation between 'union matters' and 'non-union matters'. The fact is, so many of the factors affecting the efficiency of the business – pay, hours, staffing, flexibility, change, co-operation – are things in which the union is involved. If union representatives are not involved in the consultative committee then many of these vital subjects will be omitted from the discussions.

Participation at policy level

Although the value of the departmental or unit consultative committee has been more than demonstrated, we now move into an area at company and board level where little has been done in the United Kingdom. There is a need, recognised by trade unions, many employers and all three political parties, to achieve some kind of employee participation at policy level.

Companies may, therefore, be wise to carry out some experiments in participation at the highest level to demonstrate what does and does not work in practice. Experiments being undertaken include:

The company council: employee representatives meet with the board to discuss all matters affecting the company including future planning.
Investment committees: trade union representatives within the company sit on a joint committee with divisional and company directors to discuss the investment programme.
Division board employee members: two members are appointed by the division board from a list of nominations provided by the trade unions within the company.
Main board trade union members: the appointment by the board of one or two full-time trade union officials.

These are examples of what is actually happening. There are other well-founded suggestions for experiment which include:

(a) The two-tier supervisory board which is mentioned in the Bullock Minority Report.
(b) The representative consultative board where employee representatives are consulted by the managing director on matters to which they can contribute before board decisions are taken.
(c) Two directors on the main board who are ratified by a majority of employees voting. This is somewhat parallel to existing practice where many boards have one or two members who have the confidence of the City. Boards would then ensure in future that they always have two members who have the confidence of employees.

Share ownership

Finally there are the schemes to encourage people to feel part of the organisation by holding shares. The movement for wider share ownership has some enthusiastic support and there is wide experience of various methods. Wider share ownership can be effective but it is only one part of a policy which tries to make it clear that the organisation depends on both shareholders and employees. Shareholding schemes do not act as a direct incentive except in the smallest companies or where the individuals concerned are so senior they alone can significantly influence profits.

It is unwise to encourage employees with limited means to hold all their savings in the company where they work, because if the company collapses they will lose both their savings and their livelihood.

Making things happen

It is important to note that all the methods of participation outlined in this chapter are concerned with enabling employees to contribute to more effective decision-taking at every level. These methods, however, have little to do with ensuring that the decision, when taken, will be carried out at all levels with commitment and enthusiasm.

The job of helping and ensuring people implement the decision is that of the executive in local and central government and of management in industry and commerce. All the participation in the world will never remove the prime and vital duty of the leader to obtain people's commitment to the policy, and to make the resulting action happen.

15 Trade unions

Union membership exists in most large organisations in the United Kingdom today. It is not the prime job of the trade union to make industry and commerce more effective or to persuade people to give of their best to their work. This is a management responsibility. The unions can, however, encourage people to co-operate and suggest how work can be done more efficiently and how people's abilities can be better used. Alternatively, union representatives can spend time searching out possible areas of conflict with management. They can affect people's performance more drastically by encouraging the removal of unco-operation, discouraging the acceptance of change, refusing to agree to remanning of a particular plant or machine or, in the ultimate, withdrawing their labour.

In organisations where trade unions are recognised, leaders at every level must take practical steps to achieve productive management/union relations. Otherwise, they will never achieve the highest co-operation from their fellow workers.

Industrial relations do not exist for their own sake but as a means of achieving the greatest possible productiveness in the organisation for the benefit of customers or clients, the shareholders, the community and the individual employees. The proven steps towards such productive relationships are:

Recognising a relevant role for trade unions

Avoid the situation where management appears to be only concerned with profitability and its shareholders, and it is the trade unions alone who are concerned with people and the company's employees. This kind of division is unrealistic and produces the worst results. The trade unions are not subcontractors of labour. They do not employ the company's employees.

The relevant role for trade unions in the 1980s is as representatives of those who are employed, in four specific areas.

The negotiation of justice in conditions of employment

The history of justice in the Western world has been the history of an advocate for the prosecution and an advocate for the defence – a discussion of the issues from two points of view.

The union can do this job better than the personnel department. On the whole it is not good practice for the defence counsel to be employed by the prosecution, or vice versa!

This is the union's crucial role: to achieve justice, together with management, in matters such as pay, hours and fringe benefits.

Consultation

To involve employee representatives in discussion with management on all matters affecting the efficiency of the business and the co-operation of people.

The grievance procedure

If managers are to take decisions at the speed required for the present day, they will make mistakes. A grievance mechanism which can challenge these mistakes to the highest level is essential. Such a challenge, to be effective, will periodically need an advocate from outside the organisation, whose livelihood does not depend on that organisation.

Representation at national level

There is a need for the interest of employees to be represented at national level as with other interest lobbies, such as employers, manufacturers, consumers and the like. Good government of the country depends upon a multiplicity of pressures being brought to bear, not on the absence of pressure.

It will be noted that none of these roles includes the union becoming the management. Much that has gone wrong in management/union relations can be traced to management giving up managing once they have recognised unions. Where union representatives try to act as managers or supervisors, employees are inclined to join other representative bodies to fight their union, since the union has apparently assumed the role of boss not representative. It is as unrealistic to argue that the shop steward can replace the foreman as it is to say the foreman can replace the shop steward. The effectiveness of industry and commerce depends on responsible management and responsible trade union representatives – two different but complementary roles, two parts of a whole. The object is not to remove or deny the conflict that must arise, but to make conflict productive rather than destructive.

This common sense approach is set out in a joint statement by senior trade union and management leaders. (See Appendix 9).

Encouraging a responsible and relevant role

Increasingly the reality of the situation means unions operate from the bottom upwards and not from the top downwards (see Chapter 2). What affects the behaviour of trade union members in a particular organisation is more dependent on management's attitude to them rather than on who sits on the governing body of the union. It is the members of the union who will tell their officials and their representatives what they want of them and not the other way around.

Example

Any observer who spends time in many companies will note totally different trade union behaviour between one company and another, even though they are in the same trade, the same area and have the same trade unions.

The difference between them is the way the companies are managed and the attitudes of the management towards the unions.

This underlines the importance of managers taking positive steps to encourage a productive trade union response in their own organisations.

Encouraging union membership

In its most simple form the point was established 90 years ago. If management wants responsible, relevant trade unionism which realises that the future of employees depends in part on the success of the organisation, they must persuade the most responsible employees that it is part of their concern for the company and for their fellow workers to join the union, and take a lead in influencing trade union affairs. In an organisation which recognises this the first step is to encourage employees to join the union; to attend its meetings, and thirdly to put up for election for various offices. If managers say they are 'neutral' about trade unionism this is taken to mean on the shop or office floor that they are in fact against trade unionism but do not think it wise to say so.

Some argue that a high level of union membership is against management's interest. However, this is not borne out by experience. Low union membership leads to the arrival of other unions which results in inter-union competition; alternatively, the existing union will be inclined to overpress demands in order to attract and hold membership. It is in management's interest to encourage the highest possible union membership. Rightly, conscientious objections must be respected. But this is no excuse for managements which recognise trade unions to argue that they should not try and persuade workers to overcome their apathy and play a responsible part in union affairs.

The argument is sometimes raised that if the union's action is decided increasingly by the organisation's employees it is unnecessary to have an outside union. Why not go for a staff association instead? Many companies which have tried this method regret it. A staff association does not receive TUC recognition, and will always be open to attack from outside unions which can claim independence, continuing strength and national influence quite outside anything a staff association on its own could possibly offer.

Union recognition

Where unions are not recognised and where there is a sign of some desire for trade union representation, the best results appear to be achieved by managements who, at an early stage, take the initiative in opening discussions with a particular trade union, or the fewest possible number of trade unions. By moving when something between 15 and 25 per cent of people are in a union, management can have much greater influence on the type of procedural agreements adopted, the form of representation and the selection of unions. Some of the most damaging management/trade union relations have occurred in organisations where requests for union membership and recognition from 'moderate' staff have been resisted and the demand for unionisation has fallen into unrepresentative hands. Managers need to be clear about the main points they wish to see in any procedural agreement before entering negotiations.

Procedural agreements

Written procedural agreements laying down the relationship between management and the unions are necessary. They should cover procedures for settling disputes and grievance procedures. The management should start with words that state the common ground. 'It is the purpose of both management and the unions that (a) the enterprise is successful and (b) employees are treated with justice.' Thereafter the agreement should lay down the procedures of negotiation, consultation and grievance whereby these ends are achieved.

Example

A small company of 150 employees, on finding that 25 per cent of its personnel were union members, opened negotiations and tabled a detailed draft procedural agreement based on The Industrial Society's booklet, *Model Procedural Agreements*. The union also tabled a detailed draft which they favoured. All were relieved to find that the two drafts were almost identical as they were based on the same booklet!

Representatives

A system of representatives at work group level will be necessary. Any agreement with the union should include the provision of joint credentials from the union and from management for such representatives, whether they be called shop stewards, fathers of the chapel, or staff representatives (see Appendix 10). The union will make the appointments, but management must recognise that these representatives have been appointed to operate in the organisation, the success of which is management's responsibility.

Conditions of election need to be agreed, eg that representatives shall have been in the organisation for at least a year, and perhaps, that they shall be elected by ballot. There is no need to put in the controversial word 'secret'. A ballot is defined in the dictionary as secret.

If representatives are to work effectively they will need to receive information about the organisation and its progress and they will need facilities such as the use of a room where they can meet other representatives. In the case of the senior representative, he or she may need the use of a telephone. These facilities need to be discussed with the trade unions and are best laid down. But in deciding what facilities there should be, it is important to recognise that people are working representatives – their value to members and the company hinges on their being out working on the job and not being stuck in an office.

Representatives will need some brief training on their role and on the agreements they are meant to be defending (see Appendix 11).

Relations with full-time officials

Full-time officials should be invited to the organisation at regular intervals but at least once a year to talk informally about what the organisation is trying to do. Such officials can hardly be expected to take a constructive attitude if the only time they come into contact with the company is at times of dispute.

16 Young employees

Particular attention needs to be paid to young employees. They are a company's long term investment. The contribution they make is dependent on how quickly they commit themselves to their work, and what they do about it.

It is too easy to blame people for not giving more to their work and to suggest that this is because they were not trained properly in their schools. There is evidence that most young people start their working lives in a mood of enthusiasm, and learn cynicism and apathy during their first few years in employment.

It is in the interest of the company, and the young people themselves, to take special action to develop their attitude to work during the first three years of employment. This form of training and development can best be called involvement training. Neither further education colleges nor the youth training scheme can do this job as effectively as industry and commerce.

In the past, forward looking companies allocated considerable resources to youth training. If industry is not to suffer in the future there is an urgent need to put more resources again into this work.

The most effective youth training has five elements:

1 The key person in forming attitude is as always the immediate boss. Young employees should be made responsible to a permanent boss who has a team of people. This leader should be someone who believes in young people and the need to develop them. They should not be put into some youth or employee pool. Nor should they be given the messengering type of job where they are likely to be left on their own, often with insufficient to do.

2 There should be an involvement training scheme covering the first three years in the company. It should consist of:

Work experience. Most people coming from school or college do not want to do more school and college. They are keen to earn their living and it is important for them to learn that even when work is boring and dull we still have to get it done. So, for three or four days a week they should do a regular job.

Practical academic training. This may involve half a day a week on such things as report writing, effective speaking and reporting back from a meeting, the use of percentages and scales (whether in measuring liquids or in calculating wage awards), the role of unions, the elements of safe working and the economic facts of life, ie the necessity to produce the things that people need.

Character development activities. The elements of the Duke of Edinburgh Award Scheme are worth reproducing. Young employees should carry out a project to help them realise the problems of seeing a job through from beginning to end and the need to persevere. They should carry out some form of service to the community and learn the enormous power of service as a self-motivator. They should carry out something which encourages fitness. To have real application at work there is a need for a wiry toughness. They should carry out some activities which will help them overcome fear. When tasks are faced up to they are never as bad as they seem. Spare time, half a day a week, or parts of weekends, should be devoted to these development activities.

3 During the three years of the involvement training scheme young employees should be sent on some outside experience such as Outward Bound, Brathay, Sail Training or The Industrial Society's Keble conferences for young employees.

4 Young employees should be encouraged to form and organise young employee forums to which they can invite senior managers and directors to talk on what they are doing and to answer questions. This gives young employees a practical example of what they themselves can do about the lack of communication instead of sitting back and blaming others. (See Appendix 12)

5 All those who hope to become supervisors and managers should be encouraged to carry out a leadership activity. People learn leadership by practising it. Young employees cannot expect to be put in charge of people at work straight away. They can, however, be energetically encouraged to do leadership jobs in the community.

Example

A manager persuaded a young employee to go on alternate Thursdays to act as an assistant youth club leader. By the time he had learned how to persuade the boys not to rip up the green baize of the billiard tables but to occupy themselves a little more productively (and this with no powers of punishment or fine) the young man found he had learned how to persuade people to pay more attention to quality and not to take advantage of sickness absence arrangements, and how to achieve flexibility and involvement.

17 The common purpose

If any challenging enterprise is to succeed, all those involved must have a common purpose. There will be differences of opinion about what should be done and how the results of the enterprise should be shared out, and earlier chapters have dealt with how these various viewpoints can be made productive. However, over and above these differences all great leaders – among employers, in the trade union movement and in the services – have stressed the need for a common purpose.

What then is the common purpose for all of us in industry and commerce? What is it that appeals to the hearts and minds of all who work in the enterprise and binds us together rather than separates us? Many have tried to find the right words. The best definition seems to be that our common purpose is *THE CREATION OF WORTH*. Creation is a worthy activity and the whole future depends upon it. Worth is greater than wealth which people too often think is restricted to the wealthy. Worth is worthy and not worthless. In industry and commerce we do not just create profit – in any year's work we have created worth in seven forms:

1 We have created goods and services which can be expressed as the total value of sales or the added value over and above the cost of raw materials and services bought in.
2 We have created jobs which mean so much to people in terms of self-respect. At times industry may have to declare jobs redundant but only to keep others at work.
3 We have created incomes which mean more to people than handouts, however necessary handouts may be.
4 We have created resources for reinvestment in the enterprise thus providing for future generations.

5 We have created a return on the savings of a vast number of individual people both directly and through pension funds.
6 We have created exports which make it possible for people to buy imported goods in shops.
7 We have created the money to pay taxes both directly by the company and through income tax on the salaries earned. It is these taxes which pay for the teachers, nurses, local authority housing and pensions.

Example
A company in its annual report to employees points out that they paid £52½ million in tax and this would pay for 3,000 houses, or the wages of 6,000 nurses, or the annual pensions for 35,000 married couples.

There is a need to explain the vital role of profit, but it is inaccurate and unwise to fail to explain to employees and the community at large that industry and commerce are concerned with the creation of more than profit. The customers are concerned with the quality of its products and its value to them. Employees are concerned with doing a good job and obtaining an income. Shareholders must have a return on their savings. There can only be a compassionate community if we in industry and commerce produce taxes to pay for it. The limitation to doing good is the ability to produce the wherewithal with which to do good. The common purpose of creating worth for a community covers all these interests.

Methods

Having defined the common purpose we now come to ways of bringing it home to all those who work in industry and the community at large.

Employee report
Increasing numbers of companies provide all employees with a specially written report covering the results as published in the annual report but also making clear the seven areas of creation. It is useful to point out the amounts paid to shareholders as a return on savings as against the amount paid to all employees in terms of pay and fringe benefits. Most people are surprised to note that these

last two figures are in the ratio of one to ten. Also the employee report often contains the numbers of people employed in various categories, a description of the participative machinery and the statistics of absence, employee leaving and disputes.

Annual meeting
More and more companies are organising an annual meeting of employees at each location to explain the achievements of the previous year. These meetings of employees are addressed by the most senior manager on the location who has in turn been at a briefing by the chairman. Alternatively these meetings are addressed by a board member or, in many companies, by the chairman. There is always an opportunity at such meetings to ask questions. It is best held a few days after the issue of the report to employees.

Open days
Employees deeply appreciate the chance to show their families where they work and what they do. An open day on a Saturday for the office or the factory attracts many people. It gives an opportunity to show what the firm does for society in terms of jobs, goods and services, recruitment and contributions to the public person through tax payments.

Example
On a Saturday morning a director of a commercial company brought in his young son and sat him in his chair while he dealt with some urgent papers. On their way out they met the senior elected representative on the staff consultative committee. The director introduced his son and explained his presence. The committee representative said – 'I wish my son was allowed to see where I worked'.

Schools
Every opportunity should be taken to put over the vital common purpose of industry to people in schools – at prizegivings, through parent/teacher associations and by direct liaison with schools in the area.

One of the most effective well-tried methods, proven over 25 years, is the Challenge of Industry conferences run by The Industrial Society. For two days the most senior classes of the school discuss actual problems of achieving people's commitment to work. The conference is addressed by a chairman, an experienced manager and a trade unionist. Eighty per cent of the time is spent in groups of ten led by young managers and elected representatives from industry. These groups come up with answers and in so doing gain some idea of the challenge and the importance of becoming a leader at work.

The publication *A visit to a factory*, sponsored by The Industrial Society and written by Althea Braithwaite of Dinosaur Publications Ltd for six year-olds, is worth distributing to employees with young children and in local schools. It makes clear the importance of the creation of worth.

Universities
Industrial Societies organised by students have been formed at more than 50 universities in Britain. They arrange visits to offices and factories and invite managers and trade unionists to discuss the problems in industry and commerce and the answers. These are now some of the largest student organisations.

Other organisations
Every opportunity should be taken, particularly among women's groups and church organisations, to talk about the challenge of industry. The mother's outlook on work has a profound influence on the attitude of young people.

More and more companies are encouraging visits to and from schools, universities and other organisations. They are encouraging managers, supervisors and trade unionists to set aside some limited and specific time to speak to such groups.

18 Personal action

Leaders must obviously practise the policies they put over and setting an example is one of a leader's necessary activities. But setting a good example is not enough. Leaders must take the other actions mentioned in this book if results are to be achieved.

There is nothing new in what has been written here – it is just good sound common sense – yet many people feel totally frustrated in carrying out the actions that are needed. There is, therefore, one other necessary requirement: the personal action of the individual leader.

It is always so tempting to say 'It's all too difficult, or too big', or 'I can't do anything because my senior management won't let me'. Such remarks are heard only too often among middle management in organisations where the senior management are complaining that the people in the middle will not take action on their own account.

Forbid me if you dare!

Effective leaders do not just understand about the required actions of leadership, and then wait for those above to put them into effect. If they do they may wait for ever and end up more frustrated than when they began. Nor is it wise to go to one's boss and ask for permission to carry out such things as delegating more or setting targets. Bosses often find it difficult to say yes. They worry if one subordinate takes an action – what will be the effect on the others? What would head office say?

Effective leaders tell the boss what they are going to do and why, and then look them in the eye as if to say 'Now forbid me if you dare'. If, as leaders, we are prepared to bear the responsibility for our actions ourselves, we will be surprised at how seldom we are prevented from carrying them out.

Persuading one's boss is an essential part of being a successful leader. The secret is to sell one's proposed actions in terms which are relevant to the objectives of the boss – not in terms of one's own objectives.

Example

A person was sacked from a job because her managing director said her work in developing people was irrelevant to that part of the firm which was concerned with making profits from a particular product.

The fault lay entirely with the subordinate who had failed to explain her actions in terms of their contribution to profitability.

What can I do about it?

Of course, if action depends on someone above us or alongside us doing something it will not be in our total power to bring it about. The question to ask oneself continually is not 'What can they do about it?' but 'What can I do about it?' It is no good blaming the Government, or the education system or the unions. The key question is what can I do to increase my effectiveness and the effectiveness of the people for whom I am responsible?

It is argued that change and training can only begin at the top and nothing can be done until that has occurred. This is rubbish. Almost every company started management training initially with supervisors or in the middle ranks. Thereafter, the training spread upwards. There is, in fact, no better way to start being more effective than in one's own area.

Begin where I can

Is there a logical place to start taking action? No – so long as the action one takes is part of a total leadership plan. Begin at the point that is easiest at the time. If, for instance, the organisation is worrying about communication then start with Team Briefing. We do not need first to argue that the structure must be put right before Team Briefing can begin. Having got briefing going efficiently the shortcomings of the structure will soon become apparent, and after that so will the need to train supervisors. Do not necessarily start by trying to train people.

Example

Directors of one company in 1952, after visiting America, wanted action on communication. In those days no one knew what to do about it. So on the principle that it couldn't do any harm, all the foremen were given courses on effective speaking and running meetings. Thereafter frustrated foremen wandered about the company looking for meetings to run and occasions for speaking effectively.

Far better, start by explaining and then requiring people to carry out the discipline of Team Briefing. The training need will then become obvious.

Setting myself a limited target and monitoring it

Not everything can be changed overnight. There is a need therefore to set ourselves limited, but progressive targets and to write them down with the date by which we expect to have made some significant progress. The date is essential so that progress can be monitored. Just because we have decided on something it does not mean that it will happen. There is a need to check.

Need for hope

Those who have the job of obtaining the co-operation of others must always retain hope. Hope is not to be confused with blind optimism, but if there is no hope the situation is hopeless. This means that leaders must restrain themselves from 'crying on parade'. A chairman of a company has said: 'There is no level of poor performance which cannot be reached by a person or a group of persons given sufficient lack of encouragement'.

Where is the strength to come from?

This dependence on one's own action requires a great deal of inner strength. Where is this to come from? To get on with the job, to not give up or be put off by failure, to communicate hope and enthusiasm for the task, to live with uncertainty, to believe in people and not mind being let down by others – all this requires great energy and strength. Effective leaders must find this strength somewhere. They may receive it from religious conviction or from the example of others who succeed in achieving people's fullest co-operation.

When things are difficult one can be helped by the remark of a highly successful managing director. She said:

'When you've been married to a waterman all your life you know the tide does not only turn at high water – it also turns at low'.

Great strength can be obtained by remembering the importance of what each of us as a leader is trying to do. Not only does profitability and efficiency depend on our being more effective in 'setting people alight' and getting them going; there is also a wider importance. Industry and commerce and the public services are in the business of serving people. Without the worth and service produced there would be no schools, no medical service, no help for the aged or for the starving parts of the world. Therefore, a second driving force can be found in seeing one's job in terms of service to the community. Writing in *The Apprentice of British-Westinghouse magazine* in 1919, the principal of what is now UMIST said: 'Industry, indeed, exists to create wealth for the community. It is one of the most important branches of social service. To increase the wealth of the community to which one belongs is a fine and noble aim.'

There is no long-term self-motivator greater than service and there can be few challenges more worthy than this for, 'He who makes two blades of grass grow where one grew before is doing the work of the Creator'.

Thirdly, there is the privilege and reward to be found in enthusing men and women through involving them in their work. Considerable strength can be obtained by realising that by carrying out leadership actions based on people's needs – to care, to be involved and to be needed – the working lives of all those we influence are made rather more worthwhile.

But perhaps the most exciting thought of all is to see our place in history at the end of the twentieth century. At different times in a country's history different groups of people hold the key to the future development of that society. In times of war it may be those who give their lives as soldiers, sailors and airmen. At other times it may be the politicians or the teachers, or the trade unions.

But today, the key to the future lies with those of us whose job it is to involve people in their work. Politicians, priests, trade union leaders, the media, and teachers can help if only they will. But we have the opportunity – we have people round us 35 hours a week. And we shall fulfil our place in history if we carry out the common sense actions contained in this book with humility, courage and hope.

APPENDIX I

Accountability chart

Example of part of the accountability chart used in The Industrial Society

This accountability chart covers directors, staff in Salary Groups A to F and some others. It shows how the organisation fits together.

Such a chart has many advantages in clarifying how we are linked together and who is responsible for what. However, it is damaging if people read into it more than is there and, in particular, try to compare such things as status and level.

The chart should in no way be allowed to alter the informal friendliness on which the Society is built and under which everybody should talk to anybody else about how they can better achieve the objectives of the Society.

Eric Molyneux   —Division Director
│
├ John Allen   —Head of Communication Department
│ ├─David Boot   —Section Leader
│ ├─Garth Allan   —Associate Adviser
│ ├─Mark Meeson   —Associate Adviser
│ ├─Jenny Davenport   —Associate Adviser
│ ├─Rita Kluwe   —Adviser
│ ├─Liz McCaw   —Admin Officer & Sec to HOD
│ ├─Robert Shiers   —Adviser
│ ├─Oliver Smith   —Adviser (seconded)
│ └─John Vellum   —Adviser
│
├ Caroline Blaazer   —Head of Information Technology Department
│ ├─Joanne Titmarsh   —Admin Officer & Sec to HOD
│ ├─Valerie Lowman   —Adviser
│ ├─Nicholas Pizey   —Adviser
│ └─Jeremy Wills   —Adviser
│
├ Liz Formby   —Computer Project Leader
│ ├─Clare Bevan   —Computer Training Assistant
│ ├─Simon Curtis   —Computer Systems Assistant
│ └─Lisa Jackley   —Personal Assistant to Division Director
│
├ Andrew Marx   —Head of City & Commercial Department
│ ├─Tim Cooper   —Adviser (Lloyds Insurance)
│ ├─Clare Dawkins   —Admin Officer & Sec to HOD
│ ├─Hellis Hill   —Adviser (Foreign Banks & Finance Houses)
│ ├─Colin Apthorp   —Adviser (Clearing Banks)
│ ├─Joy Evans   —Adviser (Finance Houses/Commodities)
│ ├─Diana Maw   —Adviser (Accountants)
│ ├─Gary Miles   —Adviser (non-Lloyds Insurance)
│ └─Peter Terrell   —Adviser (Building Societies)
│
└ Reg Penson   —Head of Eastern Region
   ├─Bob Campbell-Lamberton   —Adviser (Derbyshire)
   ├─Lance Hare-Scott   —Adviser (Nottinghamshire)
   ├─Michael Jackson   —Adviser (Suffolk, Norfolk and Cambridgeshire)
   ├─Alan Latham   —Adviser (West Hertfordshire and Buckinghamshire)
   ├─Jan Mayo   —Admin Officer & Sec to HOR
   ├─Julian Pirie   —Adviser (Leicester City)
   ├─Len Pounder   —Adviser (Leicestershire, South Lincolnshire and Northamptonshire)
   └─David Wright   —Adviser (East Hertfordshire & Essex)

APPENDIX 2

Performance coaching – basic policy

A minimal basic company policy

1. All employees shall have a discussion at least once a year with their manager about their performance. The discussion should recognise the areas in which the individual's performance is good and enable the person to recognise with the help of the manager the action needed to make it better.
2. The line manager is responsible for seeing that this is done.
3. Practice may vary from unit to unit but the following minimum standard shall be met:

    (a) The discussion shall be between the individual and the manager and shall take place annually.
    (b) In preparation for the interview the individual and/or the manager shall write out their comments and these shall be available to both parties.
    (c) The conclusions of the manager after the interview shall be written on the form and individuals shall have the opportunity to add written comments if they wish.
    (d) Either then or soon after a limited number of important targets shall be set or areas of work where progress is needed during the coming year. A timetable shall be included and an indication of the progress that should be made. This will form part of the next year's review and coaching.

Appendix 3

Performance coaching – simple form

FRONT OF FORM
Year ending:

Name .... **Job Title** ....
Period covered by this review ....
A. Key areas of responsibility and targets:

Reviewer's signature ....
Date ....

BACK OF FORM
B. Job Holder's comments:

                    signed ....
                    date ....

C. Comments by Reviewer's Boss:

                    signed ....
                    date ....

D. Development Plan:

(To be completed by the reviewer)   Action:

                    signed ....
                    date ....

APPENDIX 4
Understanding the economic facts

A joint statement by trade unionists and employers for the 1980s

'As employers and trade unionists, we believe that far more can be achieved by industry and commerce if the economic facts are clearly understood. We believe that people will only be committed to their work, whether it be producing goods or providing services, if they understand the purpose of what they are doing, what their efforts achieve and where the money comes from and goes to.

Whether we work in the independent or the public sector, we must all realise that our prosperity depends upon how efficiently we can produce the goods and services which people demand and that our jobs and incomes ultimately depend upon the successful performance of the organisation for which we work.

Some companies have already experienced the benefits of putting before their employees the economic facts of their business, such as the value added by each employee, investment plans, cash-flow and profits; and how these are affected by inflation, productivity levels and competition. But many companies have made no effort to do this. It is vital that everyone understands these economic facts and not solely our managers and representatives.

We believe that the most effective means of getting people to understand the economic facts is through open, honest and regular explanation of the company's own financial progress, performance and prospects.

Our experience shows that if the facts are to be believed, and if those who give them are to be trusted, the information must be:

- Regular: not just at a time of crisis or in the context of annual negotiations
- Honest: the facts, both good and bad
- Open: to *all* employees, not just to management and representatives, and with a chance to ask questions
- Relevant: primarily about the local unit for which employees work and whose performance they can directly affect.

The following checklist sets out the proven methods of communicating economic facts to employees. No one method alone is sufficient; a combination of many methods, both written and face-to-face, is required if the understanding and commitment is to be gained which will lead to greater benefits for all.

We urgently commend all companies and other organisations to take action to implement and improve their use of these methods during the 1980s.'

Signed by:

Sir Richard Cave
Chairman, Thorn EMI Ltd

Tony Hill
Chairman, Unilever UK
Holdings Ltd

Trevor Holdsworth
Chairman, GKN Ltd

Sir Hector Laing
Chairman, United Biscuits Ltd

Sir Raymond Pennock
Chairman, BICC Ltd

David Basnett General Secretary,
General and Municipal Workers Union

Sir John Boyd General Secretary,
Amalgamated Union of Engineering
Workers

Frank Chapple General Secretary,
Electrical, Electronic,
Telecommunications and Plumbing Union

Moss Evans General Secretary,
Transport and General Workers Union

Roy Grantham General Secretary,
Association of Professional, Executive,
Clerical and Computer Staffs

Here are some methods which have already proved effective:

Mass Methods

1 Annual presentation to employees

An annual presentation by the chief executive or the head of the operating unit in person to all employees on the performance of the company and of the local unit so that all employees receive the same message. This presentation is often linked to the publication of the annual employee report.

2 Audio visual programmes

Video, film or tape/slide presentation for all employees on the performance of the company, with a senior manager present to explain the contribution at local level and to answer questions.

3 Illustrated employee report

A simple written and illustrated statement for all employees at least annually on the performance at group, company and local level, explaining what was or was not achieved in the past, and outlining plans for the future.

4 Other written information

Regular newsletters to provide information on progress and achievement as well as simple explanations of economic facts.

5 Presentations to management

Six-monthly or annual presentations by the chief executive of the organisation to senior management, or to senior management and senior employee representatives explaining the company's performance and prospects.

Involving the work group

6 Team Briefing

Monthly team briefings at every level of the business for the communication and explanation of local progress and achievement by the team leader, particularly the team's own contribution and performance.

Involving Representatives

7 Presentations to trade unions

Six-monthly presentation on the company's performance and future plans to shop stewards and the full time officials involved with the enterprise.

8 Involvement of representatives

Regular discussion on company performance and operating issues with employee representatives whether through consultative committees, employee councils or other forms of joint representation, providing full opportunity for representatives to contribute.

Training

9 For supervisors, managers and representatives

Training courses for managers, supervisors and representatives, jointly wherever possible, to help them to understand how their business works and to encourage joint discussion on the action that can be taken to achieve improvements.

3 Involve all the team and encourage questions.
4 Add local information relevant to team. These will include:
Progress of the team's achievements during the past month
Plans forward
Matters affecting the *people* in the team
Your own *personal message* to your team
Points for *action*

APPENDIX 5

Management brief and pro forma for briefers

An example of a management brief where the message must be passed through three or more levels

Management brief

Department/Section .... Name of Briefer ....

Those absent .... Date and Time ....

Item and key points	**Notes by Briefers giving examples and answers to possible questions**

Notes for those briefing their teams:

1 Plan in advance what you want to say – keep it brief. Note examples (egs) which illuminate the point.
2 Keep to the point. Brief in own words and keep it simple.

3 Involve all the team and encourage questions.
4 Add local information relevant to team. These will include:
Progress of the team's achievements during the past month
Plans forward
Matters affecting the *people* in the team
Your own *personal message* to your team
Points for *action*.

APPENDIX 6

Decision-taking

Example of a policy statement

1 The organisation policy on decision-taking is based on the principle that the most highly motivated decisions will be those which an individual takes personally. Therefore wherever possible decisions will be delegated to the *individual* who has to carry out the action.

2 Where a decision is to be taken which affects a number of people it is the job of the leader of that group to take the decision *after* consulting them. The solution will then be based on what he or she believes to be right, having taken into account the views expressed, and personal experience and judgement.

3 The decision-taker will explain the 'why' of the decision to help people live with it and carry it out enthusiastically even though they may not agree with it.

4 Where a decision which affects people has been taken at a higher level it is the responsibility of the leader at each level to support it and see that it is carried out energetically whether he or she agrees with it or not.

5 When taking decisions, the guiding principle will be the greatest possible achievement of the objectives of the organisation. The decision-taker will try to be as positive and consistent as possible. If events show the decision was wrong, the decision-taker will be prepared to admit it was a mistake and will change the decision accordingly.

6 Where people believe the decision involves a gross injustice and not merely a difference of opinion they are encouraged to make use of the grievance procedure, or after talking to their immediate leader to go and see the level above.

APPENDIX 7

Joint statement by trade unionists and employers

Competitiveness with justice – our joint goal

'At this time when jobs and the standard of living in this country depend on our ability to compete worldwide and create the things that people need, we wish to state that there is an essential role, both for the management to lead the enterprise and for trade unions to represent their members. There are a number of key objectives that both have in common.
- To involve the talents of all employees at work
- To provide employment and create new jobs
- To create the goods and services that society needs
- To produce a surplus which will ensure future investment
- To create the exports vital to a trading nation's economy
- To treat people with justice at work

We urgently commend all employers and trade unionists to take action to improve management/union relations.'

Signed by:

John Harvey Jones
Chairman
Imperial Chemicals Industries plc

Sir Christopher Hogg
Chairman
Courtaulds plc

Roger Hurn
Chief Executive and Managing Director
Smiths Industries plc

The Lord Pennock
Chairman
BICC plc

Ray Buckton
General Secretary
Associated Society of Locomotive Engineers and Firemen

Gavin Laird
General Secretary
Amalgamated Union of Engineering Workers

Leif Mills
General Secretary
Banking, Insurance and Finance Union

David Plastow
Managing Director and Chief Executive
Vickers plc

George Turnbull
Managing Director
Inchcape plc

Ron Todd
General Secretary Elect
Transport and General Workers' Union

Alan Tuffin
General Secretary
Union of Communication Workers

Les Wood
General Secretary
Union of Construction, Allied Trades
and Technicians

What action can be taken?

Listed below are some of the actions that can lead to more productive management/union relations. These can be used as a starting point for discussions within companies or as a basis for the development of an organisation's own joint statement.

Management Action

Roles and recognition of responsibilities
Recognise their employees' right to belong to an independent trade union
Recognise a representative trade union for negotiating purposes
Encourage employees to belong to a trade union when recognised

Consultation and change
Consult the trade union(s) before deciding upon changes which affect their members. Enable employees to participate in the formulation of relevant management policies

Standards and discipline
Recognise the role for trade union members to improve management decisions by questioning them and to seek equitable treatment for their members. Uphold management/union agreements

Communication
Provide all employees with regular information about the performance and plans for their unit and the enterprise
Communicate regularly with trade union representatives
Communicate during negotiations according to an agreed procedure

Training and coaching
Develop the professional competence of managers in handling industrial relations issues

Greater productivity and more jobs
Be efficient, inventive and ingenious in expanding the scope for real jobs

Trade Union Action

Roles and recognition of responsibilities
Recognise the responsibility of management to concern themselves with the interest of all employees
Seek to resolve inter-union disputes
Reflect the views of their members, seeking to involve all of them through effective procedures

Consultation and change
Accept the challenge of proper consultation and share the responsibility for developing the correct policies for change, by making suggestions and using the knowledge of their members to make the operation more successful

Standards and discipline
Accept management responsibility to maintain standards of performance and orderly behaviour. Uphold management/union agreements

Communication
Recognise management responsibility for regular face-to-face communication with employees
Communicate regularly with both union members and full-time officials

Training and coaching
Make sure that the representatives are fully aware of their responsibilities and are competent to deal with industrial relations issues

Greater productivity and more jobs
Give commitment to the success of the enterprise. Work for the creation of more jobs.

APPENDIX 8

Letter acknowledging the election of a newly appointed shop steward or union representative

Dear
The company has been told that you were elected as shop steward for the ...... department on the ..... for a period of one year. A shop steward's job is an important one and this letter is written with the object of helping you to do the job well.

Enclosed is a copy of the procedure agreement between the company and the union. This will be explained to you, but if you are in any doubt about the interpretation of this agreement, please consult one of your branch officials or the personnel department.

The agreement has been in operation for many years and has proved to be satisfactory and reliable. You are, therefore, expected both by the company and the union to see that the steps laid down are carried out correctly, and, by your example, to see that the members you represent also adhere to the agreement.

The agreement lays down that you should not leave your work without the permission of your supervisor and that you must only act for the section or department for which you have been appointed. The agreement also states that you will be assured of the maintenance of your average earnings for time spent in carrying out your duties as a shop steward/union representative and that action taken by you in good faith as a shop steward/union representative will in no way affect your employment with the company.

Signed on behalf of the company:

APPENDIX 9

Checklist: action for organisations to maximise human resources

Effective leadership

An important step in maximising human resources is to ensure that the person in charge is an effective leader of a team.

1. Is there an accountability chart which defines who is responsible for motivating whom? Are spans of control wide enough to encourage delegation and small enough to motivate effectively, ie between four and fifteen people responsible to each boss?
2. Are supervisors given adequate status and authority to play an active leadership role in the organisation, to maintain standards of performance and timekeeping, and to deal initially with grievances and issues?
3. Are supervisors an integral part of the management team, having their pay and other conditions of employment based on the same principles as managers? Are their earnings ten per cent above the average of the top quarter of the people they supervise?
4. Is there a system of target setting throughout the organisation? Are the objectives of the organisation and the department clearly set down in writing and understood by all managers and supervisors?
5. Are individuals consulted before their targets are set and do they discuss how they can improve their performance with their boss?
6. Have all managers, including supervisors, received instruction on what they should do to motivate people? Is this training action-centred and practical?
7. Is there a development plan? Is it reviewed at least every two years to relate to current and future needs of people of different calibre?
8. Is there a forum where managers and supervisors can meet informally and discuss ways of improving performance?
9. Is there a known promotion procedure? Are jobs advertised within the company?

Adequate Communication

10. Is there a system of Team Briefing whereby team leaders at every level gather together each month the group responsible to them to go over what is happening and why, as it affects the group concerned?
11. Do existing arrangements enable supervisors to stop the job or bring people in so they can talk with all their working team?
12. Is the downward briefing system reinforced by written material, eg a newsletter?
13. Are noticeboards kept up-to-date? Is there an urgent board where notices only remain for 48 hours?
14. Is a full explanation given to new employees, and to existing employees who are transferred, to enable them to understand their job, their place in the organisation, how their pay is arrived at, their prospects and similar matter?
15. Is there a handbook on conditions of service, and is it kept up to date?
16. Is any check made to ensure important information is getting through and being understood?
17. Is there an upward communication mechanism of departmental consultative committees based on union-evolved representatives in those areas where unions are recognised for negotiation?
18. Do the committees have fewer than sixteen people on them and does each representative at departmental level represent no more than 100 people? Are supervisors included among the management representatives?
19. Are the committees given regular information about the organisation's trading position, finances, personnel statistics, future plans and prospects so they can make a positive contribution?
20. Is 70 per cent of a consultative committee's time spent on items put forward by management to seek the views and advice of representatives before decisions are taken or changed?
21. Should we introduce one or two quality circles on a trial basis?

Relevant conditions of employment

22. Have steps been taken to prevent earnings fluctuation? Is there a system for recognising outstanding effort?
23. Are we getting rid of mechanical means of employee control such as clocking both on the payroll and on the staff?

24 Are junior managers and supervisors involved in reviewing the pay of those for whom they are responsible?
25 Are individuals told the reasons why pay increases have been granted, or not?
26 Is there a job evaluation scheme? Are there known wage and salary structures?
27 Are steps being taken to reduce irrelevant differences between manual and non-manual grades with the object of moving towards single status?
28 Are catering facilities, lavatories and other physical conditions up to the level of new local authority housing? Is there a policy about canteen subsidies?
29 Are all other employee services reviewed at least every two years to ensure they aid high performance and are relevant to the current social situation?
30 Is there a redundancy policy? Will it help rather than hinder flexibility and job movement among employees, and meet changes in conditions and technology?

Productive management-union policies

31 Has the management thought through policies for achieving the most productive form of unionisation? Are employees aware of these policies? Where a union is recognised is there a published agreement and are employees encouraged to attend meetings and participate in the union?
32 Are there published negotiation agreements which set out the common purpose of making the organisation succeed, and of treating employees with justice? Does the agreement set out the role of management and unions in such matters as the settlement of conducting employment, discipline, dismissal, redundancy?
33 Are there published procedures which involve the union representative in the settlement of disputes, grievances and the achievement of change?
34 Are facilities provided during working hours for the election of employee union representatives? Are the representatives seen by management on appointment and provided with letters of recognition? Do they receive brief training to enable them to perform their role effectively?
35 Is there an effective procedure for announcing through union representatives and supervisors the results of negotiations?

36 Does management regularly bring together representatives of the various unions in the company to develop a common outlook and interest in the company's problems and plans?
37 Does management periodically talk to full-time union officials about matters affecting the company and its progress, and not regard the officials' function as one of appearing only at times of trouble? Do discussions cover plans for investment, development and possible closures?

Development of young people

38 Do training policies exist which cater for the particular needs of involving the young employee in work? Are young people encouraged to avail themselves of training facilities beyond those provided by the company, eg day/block release courses at local technical colleges?
39 Is it company policy to prepare young people for early responsibility?
40 Does the company have well-developed contacts with schools to enable it to meet manpower needs, eg is there a planned intake of school-leavers covering a wide range of jobs over the next few years?
41 Is there a young employees' forum to enable this group to discuss ways of improving techniques and performance, and is there provision for their recommendations to be considered by management?
42 Are young employees confident that they are following a training programme individually tailored for each of them? Are they aware of their progress or otherwise?
43 Has management sent, or is it planning to send, at least the most promising young employees on involvement training courses or conferences?
44 Can young people see their possible future line of development and salary pattern reasonably clearly?

Women

45 Is there a policy for giving women greater opportunities to use their gifts at higher levels in the company?
46 Are there 'way through' jobs for women whereby they qualify for consideration for managerial positions?

47 Do we send women of potential on courses such as The Industrial Society's Pepperell course so they can see what more they could do to contribute to the organisation and develop their abilities for work?

Appendix 10
Practical participation

The participation and involvement of people in their work will increase the effectiveness of industry and commerce in creating the goods and services the community needs. Genuine participation is also vital to meeting the needs and expectations of people at work, and it is highly relevant to any discussions on real democracy in industry. Practising managers and trade unionists, however, agree that participation is most real on the job and in day-to-day working life.

Participation at job level

Work groups
Keep the size of the work group down to a number which allows people to participate as a team. This is usually less than fifteen.

Leadership training
Train team leaders at every level in what they must do to encourage the participation of each individual and of the team as a whole – by delegation to individuals, briefing performance and decisions, asking the views of the team before decisions are taken, and encouraging people to put forward ideas and suggestions in day-to-day discussion.

Job design
Design jobs so that wherever possible individuals complete the job and take their own decisions.

Employee understanding
Encourage and equip all employees and their representatives to understand their positive role in participative arrangements – joining unions, attending meetings and standing for office.

Participation in management decisions

Team Briefing
Inform employees at every level, through regular team meetings, of matters which affect them, including operational performance and the reasons behind decisions.

Consultative committee at unit level
Ensure that there are committees at unit or departmental level where the head of the unit consults employee representatives before decisions are taken which affect them. Such committees should give an opportunity for problems to be worked at jointly. Where a trade union is recognised, the representatives should be elected by union electoral procedure.

Consultative council at company level
Ensure that there are councils which involve all employees, through their representatives, before any changes are made in company policies affecting them, and which seek their help in improving decisions and policies. Where trade unions are recognised for negotiation these are union representatives.

Extension of negotiation
Recognise trade unions and widen the scope of negotiation to cover policies for planning and major change under which management should operate. Make clear in joint agreements that unions, employers and employees all share a common purpose in the success of the enterprise and the just treatment of all employed.

Equal opportunity
Ensure that policies give those most able to participate as managers the opportunity to be promoted.

Single status
Encourage participation by developing common conditions of employment.

Participation in company policy

Annual report to employees
Hold a meeting of all employees in the unit (less than 500) once a year where the senior executive, or someone briefed by that person, explains the results of the company and talks about its plans. Also provide an annual report to employees which gives company results and other information such as numbers employed, labour turnover, safety record, etc.

Union/board meeting
Where trade unions are recognised for negotiation the board should meet senior representatives and full-time union officials at least once a year to discuss the company's progress and future plans, including plans for investment, mergers and closure.

Experiments at board level
Experiment during the next five years with various methods which enable employees to influence policy decisions at board level. Try having:
- (a) two directors on a unitary board whose appointment is ratified by employees
- (b) a group of elected employee representatives advising the board; where trade unions are recognised for negotiation these should include the union representative
- (c) an agreement negotiated between employers and employee representatives which gives employees the opportunity to influence decisions at board level

Immediate action

Participation conference
Discuss with representatives of every group of employees at participation conferences and in other ways their views on the action needed to achieve practical participation.

Participation policy
Formulate and publish a participation policy.

Training
Train managers and representatives in the relevance and practice of participation. Where unions are recognised the training of both groups is best carried out in conjunction with the trade unions.

Government action

The Employment Act 1982 section 2 requires companies to report annually what they have done to encourage employee participation.

Legislative action could usefully include items 6, 7, 11 and require experiments at board level by large companies as in 13.

Appendix II

The Industrial Society – objectives

The Industrial Society aims to promote the fullest involvement of all people in their work, in order to increase the effectiveness of organisations and the satisfaction of individuals in creating the prosperity the community needs.

The Society's work concentrates on six main areas:
- developing effective leadership at all levels
- extending proven methods of communication and consultation
- operating productive management/union relations
- establishing relevant conditions of employment
- developing young people for work and at work
- achieving greater recognition of the importance of creating prosperity through industry and commerce

The Society carries out this work in the United Kingdom, and, where this can be done without prejudice to the Society's work in the United Kingdom, in developing countries.

Effective leadership

The Society works for effective leadership in organisations by advocating that:

(a) Managers at all levels should understand their vital role in securing the co-operation of people at work in order to achieve better results.

(b) All leaders should be trained in the actions they need to take to ensure individuals working in teams contribute the maximum to the task.

(c) The structure of an organisation should show each leader's accountability for the involvement of not more than fifteen individuals.

(d) All people at work should have clearly defined and attainable targets which are reviewed by their managers on a regular basis.

(e) People in the most senior positions should ensure there is adequate leadership training, clear structures and systematic communication.

Communication and consultation

The Society seeks to increase the involvement of people in their work by:

(a) Implementing effective and systematic communication procedures to ensure managers explain to employees all matters which affect them at work, and by ensuring leaders brief their teams regularly about plans and achievements.
(b) Developing systematic consultative procedures to give employees the opportunity to put forward their views while decisions which affect them are still in the formative stage.
(c) Encouraging the provision of relevant financial information to explain to employees the performance and the needs of the organisation.
(d) Urging all employees in the organisation to appreciate the vital common purpose of the creation of prosperity.
(e) Promoting a wider understanding of the need for continuing technological change and encouraging people to respond to the need for new skills and work practices.
(f) Training people at all levels in practical communication skills needed in the effective operation of communication and consultation procedures.

Productive management/union relations

The Society works for productive management/union relations, by:

(a) Achieving the positive recognition, acceptance and understanding at all levels by both managers and trade unionists of the essential role of the other party.
(b) Advocating that managers and trade unionists should encourage people to play an active and responsible part in the democratic machinery of their union.
(c) Promoting orderly industrial relations between managers and trade unionists through clear and effective agreements.
(d) Training managers and shop stewards to understand their respective roles through separate and joint training.
(e) Encouraging trade unionists to seek greater inter-union co-operation at the place of work.
(f) Providing practical guidance to all parties on how they can

achieve effective communication during negotiation.
(g) Encouraging managers and trade unionists to develop joint discussions to enable each to contribute to increasing productivity.

Relevant conditions of employment

The Society works for conditions of employment which result in high performance. It emphasises:

(a) Remuneration which provides non-fluctuating basic earnings in accordance with agreed and published pay structures.
(b) The progressive removal of irrelevant and arbitrary differences in status between groups of people at work.
(c) The need for employers to take action to ensure women contribute to and receive greater satisfaction from working life.
(d) The need for physical working conditions which protect the health and safety of people at work, and for medical and catering facilities which contribute to this.
(e) The need to reduce the length of the average working week without any increase in unit cost.

Young people and work

The Society works for the training and development of young people at work. It aims to:

(a) Ensure that all young people at work are trained and developed to put more effort into and get more satisfaction out of their work.
(b) Provide opportunities for young people to understand the challenge of managing and representing people at work.
(c) Encourage opportunities for young people of mixed abilities to work together and respect the contribution each makes to the task.

Education for Industrial Society

The Society campaigns for greater understanding of the importance of creating prosperity through industry and commerce. It achieves this objective primarily by supporting a sister organisation, Education for Industrial Society, which aims to:

(a) Encourage the community to understand and communicate the vital contribution that industry and commerce make to society by creating prosperity.

(b) Achieve a more relevant preparation for working life, an understanding of the opportunities that exist and the skills needed in industry and commerce.

(c) Provide opportunities for young people in the course of their education to understand the challenges of managing and representing people at work.

(d) Help teachers understand the task of industry, and industry to understand the task of teaching establishments.

(e) Develop Student Industrial Societies at universities and colleges of higher education.

(f) Campaign for practical training and employment opportunities for unemployed young people.

APPENDIX 12

Sources of examples given in text

The points made in this book are based in particular on the experiences and observations in the following organisations:

Amalgamated Union of Engineering Workers
Anglo-American Corporation
C T Bowring & Co Ltd
British Leyland Motor Corporation
British Visqueen Ltd
Cadbury Schweppes plc
Cadillac Motor Car Division, Detroit
Cantrell and Cochrane Ltd
Chance Brothers Ltd
Charrington and Co plc
Civil Service
Deloitte & Co Ltd
Delta Metal Co plc
Dowty Group plc
English Electric Co Ltd
Esso Petroleum Co plc
Fleetlands RN Aircraft Yard
Ford Motor Co plc
Ford Werke, Cologne
GEC Machines Ltd
Glacier Metal Co Ltd
Greenall Whitley and Co Ltd
Hardy Spicer Ltd
H J Heinz Co plc
Alfred Herbert Ltd

Hoover plc
ICI Nobels Explosive Co Ltd
ICI plc: Plastics Division
    Mond Division
    Organics Division
    Wilton Works
John Laing and Son plc
John Leinst & Co Ltd
Marks & Spencer plc
National Coal Board
Ocean Steam Ship Co Ltd
Philips Electrical plc
Pilkington Brothers plc
Reed International plc
Rists Wires & Cables Ltd
Royal Naval Dockyards
Shell Chemical Co plc
Smiths Industries plc
Steel Plants, Durgapur
Talbots plc
Transport and General Workers' Union
Ushers Wiltshire Brewery
Vickers plc
Wates Ltd
Whitbread & Co plc
Yorkshire Imperial Metals Ltd

Appendix 13

Sources of inspiration

People whose thoughts and ideas have particularly influenced the author include:

Alan Abbot
Dr John Adair
Ernie Allen
William Allen
Malcolm Anson
Peter Balfour
Dick Banks
Reg Banister
David Pritchard Barrett
Sir James Blair-Cunynghame
Oliver Blanford
Joshua Bottomley
Peter Bottomley
Virginia Bottomley
Cecillia Bottomley
Sir John Buckley
Frank Burr
Sir Richard Cave
Michael Clarke
Julia Cleverdon
Alan Cooper
Russell Currie
George Daffern
Duke of Edinburgh Study Conference 1956
R E England
John England Crowther
Lord Feather
Sir Monty Finneston
Lord Fleck
Andrew Forrest
Bridget Gardiner
Barbara Garnett
Christopher Garnett
Dr Maxwell Garnett
William Garnett
Ron Gibb
Derek Gladwin
Win Gode
Ted Grint
Pat Hobson
John Humble

Lord Hunt
Alfred Inglis
Alec Irvine
Heather Jackson
Sir Alex Jarratt
E H L Jennings
Jack Jones
Gordon Lambsdale
Nicola Mardall
Normal McCleod
Sander Meredeen
Andrew Moffat
Bill Morgan
Trevor Owen
Jim Palmer
John Parker
Rev David Partridge
Sir John Partridge
Dr Bill Paul
Elizabeth Pepperell
W H Perkins
David Plastow
Dr Christopher Poulton
Rex Roberts
Dr Alan Robertson
C G Robinson
Frank Rogers
Andy Sargent
Sammy Saunders
Stan Shepherd
Lord Sieff
Bertram Simpson, Bishop of Southwark
Elvie Storey
John Stuart
Rosalind Swift
Tim Vidal-Hall
Neil Wates
John Watts
Bob Wessell
Mrs Woodward-Fisher

INDEX

Accountability charts 28, 107-8,
  see also Responsibility
Achievement
  sense of 17, 71
  targets 38-9
Action
  achieving objectives, 15-6
  carrying out decisions 57, 86
  Leadership 31-2, 101-5
Action-centred leadership 30
Adair, John 30
Assessment of performance 39, 45
Attitude surveys 81
Authority
  leaders' 57
  line of 18, 21, 26, 28
  questioning 6, 11

Ballots 92
Boards (committees) 85
Bonus schemes 8, 9, 73
Boring jobs 6, 41, 69
Braithwaite, Althea 100
Brathay 94
Briefing *see* Team briefing
Budget 49
Bullock Minority Report (1977) 85

Challenge of Industry Conferences (Industrial Society) 99
Change
  acceptance of 75
  cooperation 42, 45, 122
Committee
  encouraging 31, 86
  incentives 9
  to work 2, 3, 4, 5
Committee of Inquiry on Industrial Democracy (1977) 85
Communication
  between levels 76, 79-80
  briefing 41, 56, 102
  checklist 128
  failure 42
  method 43-4, 98-100, 115
  trade unions 123
Company councils 85
Compassionate community 1, 9, 98
Complaints 49
Computer industry 5
Conditions of employment 73-8, 88, 128-9
Conflict
  at work 89
  by misunderstanding 41
Consensus 53, 54

139

Consistency 58, 65
Consultation
  decision-taking 54, 55, 82-4
  trade unions 88, 122
Consultative efficiency committees 82-84
Co-operation
  at work 2, 19, 41, 87
  by persuasion 10, 13, 42
  decisions 53
  discipline 59, 60
  with change 42, 45, 122

Decisions 53-8, 119
  involvement 18, 133
  lowest level 27, 54, 70
  power to affect 6, 86
  representatives 18
Delegation
  decision-taking 53, 54, 57
  to deputies 26
  to individual workers 17, 32, 70, 101
Demotion 74
Departmental committees 82
Deputising 25-6
Deselection 61
Development
  high potential people 40
  leaders 34
  young employees 93-4
Discipline 22, 59-63, 122
Dismissal 60-1, 62-3
Disputes 91
Drills (procedures)
  decision-taking 54-8
  disciplinary 60
  monitoring 16
  target-setting 38
  team briefing 46
Drunk at work 63
Dual accountability 26
Duke of Edinburgh Award Scheme 94

Economic facts 113-6
Efficiency
  consultative committees 82-4
  pay 74
  people 14,19
Effort and results 16
Elections (trade unions) 92
Employment Act (1982) 135
Employment law
  disciplinary procedure 62-3
  working rights 7
Equal justice 61-2, 121
Equal opportunity 35-6, 134
Expectations of work 6
Experience at the bottom 33-4

Feedback (communication) 80
Fines 63
Flexible hours 77
Foremen and shop stewards 18, 89
Freedom and anarchy 11
Frustration
  cause of sickness, 2
  decision-taking 57
  over-protection 14
  underuse of abilities 2
Full-time union officials 92
Further education colleges 93

Gaussian distribution 16
Grapevine 43
Grievance procedure 57, 88, 91
Group decisions 53
Group technology 70

Hardship funds 78
High performance
  incentives 8, 71, 73, 74, 75
  working conditions 76
High potential 40
Hourly pay 76, 77
Hours of work 76-7

Immediate boss
  accountability charts 28
  importance 11
  must be known 18, 21
Implementing decisions 57, 86
Incentives to work
  achievement 71
  changing 7
  money 8-9, 73-5
  shareholding schemes 86
Industrial relations 87
Industrial Society 137-40
  accountability chart 107-8
  briefing courses 50-1
  Challenge of Industry Conferences 99
  Keble Conferences 94
  Pepperell Courses 36
Industrial tribunals 63
Information
  briefing 43
  decision-taking 55
  local 49
  representatives 92
Inter-union competition 90
Investment committees 85
Involvement
  lack of 12, 14
  machinery for 79-86
  over-involvement 14
  representatives 116
  training 93
  workers' 6, 41, 58, 69, 104, 133-6
Jobs
  creation 1, 2, 97, 123, 124
  descriptions 37
  design 69-71
  enrichment 70
  evaluation 74
  rotation 69

Keble Conferences (Industrial Society) 94

Language of work groups 47
Leadership
  action-centred 30
  by persuasion 18, 102
  checklist 127-31
  denigrated 11
  divided 22
  training 29-33
  young employees 94
Leadership *see also* **Team leaders**
Leisure 3
Levels of management
  number 5, 26, 80
  structure 19
Low pay 74
Loyalty to employer 7

Management-union relations 15, 87, 91, 121-4, 129-30
Manipulation 13
Matrices management 28
Membership of unions 32, 90
Middle managers 45, 101, 102
Miners' strike (1984-5) 8
Monitoring
  briefing 48, 51
  decisions 57
  procedures 16
  targets 103
  walking the job 66
Motivation
  boring jobs 6
  foreign countries 3
  service 104
  status and conditions 76-7
Moving
  to other jobs 7
  within the organisation 40

Night shifts 6

Offices
  section leaders 18

working conditions 76
Open days 99
Operational management 26
Organisational charts 28
Outward Bound 94
Overtime 77

Participation *see* **Involvement**
Pay 73-5
Pepperell Course (Industrial Society) 36
Performance
   coaching 39-40, 109, 111
   standards 37-8
Personnel matters 49
Persuasion
   at work 10, 13
   leadership function 18, 102
Piecework 73
Praise 66-7
Procedures *see* **Drill (procedures); Grievance procedure**
Productivity 42, 87, 123, 124
Profit
   centres 27, 71
   efficiency 74, 104
   motive 13
   role 98
Progress 49
Punishment 59, 60, 61, 62
Pyramidal structures 21

Quality
   control 18
   customers' requirements 98

Rat race 13, 14
Recognition of unions 90-1
Recreation 76
Redundancy 75
Representatives 44, 88, 91, 92, 116
   consultative committees 82, 84

Responsibility
   decision-taking 53-4, 55
   definition essential 18, 21, 26
   divided 22
   trade unions 123
Restrictive practices 75
Risk taking 53
Rules 59
Rumour 43

Sail Training 94
Salaries 75
School and industry 99-100
Selection of leaders 34
Service to the community 94, 104
Share ownership 85-6
Shifts
   briefing 45, 46, 47-8
   night work 6
Ship system 27-8
Shop stewards
   and employers 125
   and foremen 18, 89
   potential leaders 34
   representative function 18, 42, 44, 84, 91
Sickness absence 2, 59, 76
Size
   organisations 5, 27
   work groups 22
Staff associations 90
Staff handbook 59-60
Standard of living 1
Status (conditions of employment) 76
Stealing at work 63
Structure
   job organisation 71
   supervisory 19
Suggestion schemes 81
Supervisors
   briefing 47
   executive function 18

levels 42-3
salaries policy 75
training 102-3
Suspension (discipline) 61, 63
Targets
briefing 49
monitoring 103
setting 31, 101
work 37-9
Tax levels 9
Team briefing 41-51, 102-3, 128, 133
forms 117-8
frequency 32, 116
Team leaders
appointment 35
briefing 47
development 34
function 11, 21
selection 34
training 29-33
working bosses 23-4
Teams
leadership 11, 33
offices 76
place in structure 21
size 22, 31, 46
Teams see also **Work groups**
Thomas Aquinas, Saint 14
Time clocks 76, 77-8
Trade unions 87-91
changing role 9
consultation 55, 84-5, 116
full-time officials 92
members 32, 90
relations with management 15, 87, 91, 121-4, 129-30
roles in disciplinary procedures 61
Trade unions see also **Shop stewards**
Trade Union Congress 90
Training
leadership 29-33, 102-3, 116, 123

representatives 116, 124
staff 27
young employees 93-4
Trust 53

Unanimity 54
Underuse of people 2-3, 14
Unemployment 1, 6, 8
Unfair dismissal 61
Universities and industry 100

Wages 73-4, 76
Walking the job 32, 48, 57, 65-7, 80
Warnings 61, 62
Wealth creation 1, 13, 97
Welfare schemes 11
Welfare State 7
Women
flexible hours 77
leaders 35-6, 130-1
Work experience 94
Work groups
briefing see Team briefing
leaders 17
pools 24-5
size 22
Work groups see also **Teams**
Work study 18, 27
Working bosses 23-4
Working conditions (physical) 32, 73, 76-7
Worth creation 97
Written briefings 44

Young employees 93-5, 130
Youth training schemes 93

The Industrial Society – services

The Industrial Society is independent and self-financing and has the support of both employers and trade unions. It has 16,000 member organisations which include industrial and commercial companies, trade unions, nationalised industries, central and local government departments and employers' associations. Successful organisations in every sector of employment belong to the Society and its Council comprises 70 leaders in manufacturing industry, commerce, government and trade unions.

The Society has a record of solid achievement in helping companies improve their performance. It provides a wealth of practical benefits and is the country's leading independent advisory organisation on leadership, communication and industrial relations.

Its work and advice is practical, based on the successful examples of profitable and effective organisations. It acts as a centre for sharing experience of actions which work in practice and thereby helps members to take action themselves to achieve increased efficiency and profitability. It encourages proven techniques which are acceptable to trade unions. It campaigns among employees, in education, and the community for greater understanding of the importance of creating worth or wealth in industry and commerce.